EXPLORATIONS

STUDIES IN CULTURE AND COMMUNICATION

VOLUME 6

*Edited by Edmund Carpenter and
Marshall McLuhan*

WIPF & STOCK · Eugene, Oregon

Wipf and Stock Publishers
199 W 8th Ave, Suite 3
Eugene, OR 97401

Explorations 6
Studies in Culture and Communication
By Carpenter, E S and Easterbrook, W T
Copyright©1954, Edmund S. Carpenter & Marshall McLuhan Estates
ISBN 13: 978-1-62032-432-5
Publication date 9/29/2016
Previously published by University of Toronto, 1955

This is an anniversary new edition of the eight co–edited issues of Explorations, with annotations by Michael Darroch and Janine Marchessault, in conjunction with students and researchers at the University of Windsor and York University, Canada. Research for the annotated editions was made possible by a grant from the Social Sciences and Humanities Research Council of Canada. Additional research was provided by Lorraine Spiess in conjunction with the Estate of Edmund Carpenter. Permissions research was provided by Jonathan McKenzie. This republication project was a joint initiative undertaken by the estates of Marshall McLuhan and Edmund Carpenter.

Funding for Issues 1–6 (1953–1956) was originally provided by a grant from the Ford Foundation's Behavioral Sciences Program. Issues 7–8 (1957) were sponsored by the Telegram of Toronto.

Typography for Issue 1 was designed and printed by Rous & Mann Press Limited, Toronto. The cover of Issue 7 and the cover and typography of Issue 8 were designed by Harley Parker and printed courtesy of the University of Toronto Press. Please see individual issues for further notes on contributors and acknowledgements.

Every effort has been made to contact copyright holders and to ensure that all the information presented is correct. Some of the facts in this volume may be subject to debate or dispute. If proper copyright acknowledgment has not been made, or for clarifications and corrections, please contact the publishers and we will correct the information in future reprintings, if any.

EXPLORATIONS . . .

is designed, not as a permanent reference journal that embalms truth for posterity, but as a publication that explores and searches and questions.

We envisage a series that will cut across the humanities and social sciences by treating them as a continuum. We believe anthropology and communication are approaches, not bodies of data, and that within each the four winds of the humanities, the physical, the biological and the social sciences intermingle to form a science of man.

Volumes 1 through 6:

Editor:
    E. S. Carpenter
Associate Editors:
    W. T. Easterbrook
    H. M. McLuhan
    J. Tyrwhitt
    D. C. Williams

Address all correspondence to EXPLORATIONS
University of Toronto
Toronto, Canada

Volumes 7 & 8:

Editors:
    Edmund Carpenter
    Marshall McLuhan

Sponsor Telegram of Toronto
Publisher University of Toronto

July, 1956

Explorations, 1953–57

Foreword to the Eight-Volume Series of the 2016 Edition, Volumes 2–8

(The main Introduction to this series is in Volume One)

Michael Darroch (University of Windsor) and
Janine Marchessault (York University)

Explorations was an experimental interdisciplinary publication led by faculty and graduate students at the University of Toronto in which the media theorist Marshall McLuhan and the radical anthropologist Edmund Carpenter formulated their most striking insights about new media in the electric age. The journal served to disseminate some of the insights and experiments of the Culture and Communications graduate seminar (1953–55), an innovative media think tank of the 1950s. The eight coedited issues of *Explorations* are republished here for the first time since their original printing in the 1950s.

The Explorations research group aimed to develop a "field approach" to the study of new media and communication. While inspired by a postwar, modernist discourse of universality, no single mode of research was dominant. By their own account, the team sought "an area of mutually supporting insights in a critique of the methods of study in Economics, Psychology, English, Anthropology, and Town Planning."[1] *Explorations* published writings by group

---

1. Herbert Marshall McLuhan Fonds, held in Library and Archives Canada (LAC) in Ottawa. Further references to the McLuhan Fonds will be identified as LAC followed by the call number MG 31, D 156, the volume number, and the folder number (here: LAC MG 31, D 156, 145, 35).

members along with contributions on topics ranging from ethnolinguistics to economic theory, from art and design to developmental psychology, from psychoanalysis to nursery rhymes and bawdy ballads, from urban theory to electronic media. The journal treated culture, and cultural studies, as a landscape of experiences and knowledge. An experimental space in its own right, *Explorations* counted among its more than eighty contributors both established and emerging scholars, scientists, and artists.

The think tank and the journal were supported by a grant from the Ford Foundation's newly established interdisciplinary research and study program in behavioral sciences (most likely cowritten by McLuhan and Carpenter and assisted by the then doctoral student Donald Theall). The group obtained $44,250 for a two-year research project devoted to studying the "changing patterns of language and behavior and the new media of communication."[2] Within North America, the Toronto group's proposal can be counted among the very first attempts to combine explicitly the study of culture *and* communication. The timing of this grant is significant given the scope of contemporaneous studies of media underway in the United States and Europe: functionalist and critical cultural studies of mass communications, theories of cybernetics, studies of social interaction, as well as psychological studies of the effects of media on human perception. Carpenter, initially the driving force behind *Explorations*, acted as editor of the first six issues before becoming coeditor with McLuhan for issues 7 and 8, which were sponsored by the *Toronto Telegram*. A ninth and final issue, entitled *Eskimo* (1959), combined Carpenter's writings on indigenous art and culture of the Aivilik juxtaposed with images from filmmaker Robert Flaherty and drawings by Frederick Varley. After Beacon Press published a selection of *Explorations* contributions in 1960, coedited by Carpenter and McLuhan as *Explorations in Communication*, McLuhan later resuscitated the spirit of *Explorations* as a "magazine within a magazine," a publication inside the University of Toronto's alumni magazine, the *Varsity Graduate* (1964–72).

2. *Ford Foundation, 1953, Ford Foundation Annual Report 1953*, New York: Ford Foundation: 67. The Ford Foundation's Behavioral Sciences Program had the stated goal of "improving the content of the behavioral sciences" by specifically supporting "interdisciplinary research and study." Launched in 1952, the program aimed to help the "intellectual development of the behavioral sciences" by "improving their relationship with such disciplines as history, social and political philosophy, humanistic studies and certain phases of economics" (67).

The group's proposal to Ford's Behavioral Sciences Program is revealing of the central assumptions that would underpin the graduate seminar and *Explorations*. The proposal's point of departure is not yet an assumption about the power of media forms to shape content, but rather the understanding that methods for studying new media required recognition of new patterns emerging across technological, cultural, and urban life. Underpinning the proposal is a conversation that McLuhan in particular had started with advocates of cybernetic theories. Carpenter was also of course conversant with the writings of anthropologists who were deeply involved with developing cybernetic models and metaphors within the social sciences, among others Gregory Bateson and Margaret Mead. Cybernetic theories also came to the group through Donald Theall, who would complete his PhD dissertation in 1954 on "Communication Theories in Modern Poetry: Yeats, Pound, Joyce and Eliot" under the supervision of both McLuhan and Carpenter.

"Well aware of the brilliant new developments in communication study at Massachusetts Institute of Technology," the Ford grant explains, gesturing both to Norbert Wiener's cybernetic conferences and to Claude Shannon and Warren Weaver's mathematical theory of communication, "the undersigned propose to utilize these insights but to employ also the technique of studying the forms of communication, old and new, as art forms," an approach already "implicit in the very title of Harold Innis' *Bias of Communication*."[3] The Toronto group proposed to study the effects of new media forms on patterns of language, economic values, social organization, individual and collective behaviour, always keeping in mind accompanying changes to the classroom and the networks of city life. In their eyes the central problem consisted of two aspects. First, "the creation of a new language of vision" that "arises from all our new visual media and which is part of the total language of modern culture." Second, the Toronto group proposed to study "the impact of this total social language on the traditional spoken and written forms of expression." These two core objectives they would pursue in the pages of *Explorations* through numerous contributions. As clearly indicated in an early draft of their Ford proposal, the core research group

3. Edmund S. Carpenter, Jaqueline Tyrwhitt, H. M. McLuhan, W. T. Easterbrook, and D. C. Williams, 1953, "University of Toronto: Changing Patterns of Language and Behavior and the New Media of Communication." Ford Foundation Archives. Grant File PA 53–70, Section 1, 1–11. Rockefeller Archive Center, New York: 4.

represented the five key disciplines that would supplement each other: anthropology, psychology, economics, town planning, and English.[4]

While no one discipline was privileged above the others, anthropology played a special role in creating a strong comparative framework from the start. In addition to anthropological discussions of cybernetics, the Sapir-Whorf theory was an important intellectual foundation. As with Innis, Edward Sapir (a German-born American who spent fifteen years in Ottawa working for the Geographical Survey of Canada) offered a multifocal habit of vision, working between linguistics, anthropology, and psychology. For the grant applicants, Sapir "brought together European attitudes towards psychoanalysis (emphasis on socially-situated personality) and North American attitudes towards social structure (culture)." Moreover, Sapir "fused the European concern with philology with [the] North American concern with dynamic patterns in language."[5] The anthropologist and ethnolinguist Dorothy Lee was arguably one of the group's "most influential force[s],"[6] contributing six articles on language, value, and perception. Her insight that peoples such as the Trobrianders perceived lineal order differently from Western cultures had already been cited by Bateson and Ruesch (1951), and was central to the delineation of acoustic and visual cultures undertaken by the Explorations group, and in later studies by both McLuhan and Carpenter.

In developing their methodologies, seminar faculty and graduate students undertook a number of critical media experiments on changing patterns of perception resulting from new media. The CBC and the then Ryerson Institute placed studio space and media equipment at their disposal. The experiment tested their central hypothesis that different media (speech, print, radio, television) lend themselves to different kinds of pedagogical experiences.[7] It is surprising that such findings have never been fully taken up by educational media researchers. Hopefully, the republication of these early studies will

4. "Changing Patterns of Man and Society Associated with the New Media of Communication." Draft of Ford Foundation Proposal, likely 1953. LAC MG 31, D 156, 204, 26.

5. Carpenter et al, 1953: 2.

6. Edmund Carpenter, 2001, "That Not-So-Silent Sea," in Donald F. Theall (Ed.), *The Virtual Marshall McLuhan* (p. 240), Montreal: McGill-Queen's University Press.

7. Edmund Carpenter, 1954, "Certain Media Biases," *Explorations* 3:65–74; Edmund Carpenter and Marshall McLuhan, 1956, "The New Languages," *Chicago Review* 10(1): 46–52; Edmund Carpenter, 1957, "The New Languages," *Explorations* 7:4–21.

renew interest in the cognitive studies of media which have focussed too narrowly, according to Carpenter and McLuhan, on attention and inputs and not enough on the creative and critical aspects of perception.

What is clear in reading through the *Explorations* issues is that Carpenter and McLuhan were most interested in the new kinds of learning made possible through the media. McLuhan, in particular, was influenced by research into human perception as part of his approach to media studies since he believed that these media were altering our senses, our forms of attention and knowledge production. Carpenter and McLuhan would assert that the media are transforming the human sensorium, an idea captured perhaps most playfully in the final coedited issue, *Explorations* 8, an ode to James Joyce devoted to the oral, to the new "acoustic space" of the electric age: "Verbi-Voco-Visual." The issue features seven essays, including one by McLuhan, that explore different aspects of oral culture—mostly concerned with a transition to a new orality. Twenty-four non-authored "Items," which include some previously published essays by McLuhan and Carpenter, appear as humorous intellectual sketches exploring topics like "Electronics as ESP," car commercials, bathroom acoustics, dictaphones, and of course wine. The final "Item," number 24, entitled "No Upside Down in Eskimo Art," reiterated McLuhan and Carpenter's core assertion that "after thousands of years of written processing of human experience, the instantaneous omnipresence of electronically processed information has hoicked us out of these age-old patterns into an auditory world." In the history of media studies in Canada and internationally, the *Explorations* journal is an important starting point for defining the rich new insights around new media cultures that the Toronto School helped inaugurate.

References

Carpenter, Edmund S., Jaqueline Tyrwhitt, H. M. McLuhan, W. T. Easterbrook, and D. C. Williams. 1953. "University of Toronto: Changing Patterns of Language and Behavior and the New Media of Communication." Ford Foundation Archives. Grant File PA 53–70, Section 1, 1–11. Rockefeller Archive Center, New York.

Carpenter, Edmund. 1954. "Certain Media Biases." *Explorations* 3:65–74.

Carpenter, Edmund. 1957. "The New Languages." *Explorations* 7:4–21.

Carpenter, Edmund. 2001. "That Not-So-Silent Sea." In Donald F. Theall (Ed.), *The Virtual Marshall McLuhan* (pp. 236–61). Montreal: McGill-Queen's University Press.

Carpenter, Edmund, and Marshall McLuhan. 1956. "The New Languages." *Chicago Review* 10(1): 46–52.

Ford Foundation. 1953. *Ford Foundation Annual Report 1953*. New York: Ford Foundation.

Ruesch, Jurgen, and Gregory Bateson. 1951. *Communication, the Social Matrix of Psychiatry*. New York: Norton.

Theall, Donald. 1954. *Communication Theories in Modern Poetry: Yeats, Pound, Eliot and Joyce*. Doctoral dissertation. Toronto: University of Toronto.

Summaries of All Eight
Explorations Volumes

Explorations 1

Explorations 1 took an audaciously new approach to communications and cultural research "cutting across" studies in anthropology, literature, social sciences, economics, folklore, and popular culture. From Copernican revolutions (Bidney) to a seventeenth-century translation of Sweden's Mohra witchcraft trials (Horneck); from senses of time (Leach) to the meaning of gongs (Carrington); from Majorcan customs (Graves) to a typography of functional analysis (Spiro); from Veblen's economic history (Riesman) to contemporary stress levels (Selye), the issue also included one of György Kepes's earliest drafts on fusing "art and science," an essay on Freud and vices (Goodman), and a return to childhood in Legman's work on comic books, before concluding with now classic essays by McLuhan and Frye. The cover of *Explorations* 1 depicts a series of masks from the award-winning film *The Loon's Necklace* (Crawley Films, 1948).

Explorations 2

Explorations 2's mischievous spoof covers, both front and back, inside and outside, were labelled "Feenicht's Playhouse," a reference to the Phoenix playhouse of Joyce's *Wake*. The key playful headline, "New Media Changing Temporal and Spatial Orientation to Self," was accompanied by multiple hoax articles, including "Time-Space Duality Goes" and "TV Wollops MS," a reference to television's apparent power over manuscript culture as evidenced by the group's media experiment at CBC studios. Exemplifying the playfulness of the core faculty's discussions about new media and behaviour, it is not surprising the McLuhan would publish in this issue his now famous article "Notes on the Media as Art Forms" alongside essays by other seminar participants: Tyrwhitt resuscitated an unpublished article, "Ideal Cities and the City Ideal," a historical survey of proposals for ideal urban designs (originally drafted for the defunct journal *trans/formation: art, communication, environment*). Carpenter's "Eternal Life" is a first analysis of Aivilik Inuit concepts of time; then student Donald Theall's "Here Comes Everybody" offered a snapshot of his research on Joyce and communication theories in modern poetry; anthropologist Dorothy Lee, who would visit the seminar in March 1955, offered a review of David Bidney's challenge to scholarly traditions in his 1953 book *Theoretical Anthropology*. In addition, Carpenter fleshed out the contents with contributions from political economy, anthropology, psychology, and English: the second part of Riesman's Veblen study; Lord Raglan on social classes; Derek Savage on "Jung, Alchemy and Self"; the *New Yorker*'s Stanley Hyman on Malraux's thesis of the "museum without walls"; and A. Irving Hallowell's extended essay on "Self and its Behavioral Environment"—the inspiration for the spoof cover.

Explorations 3

Explorations 3 was initially planned as a volume dedicated to Harold Innis. In the end, the issue would only include Innis's essay "Monopoly and Civilization," introduced by Easterbrook, and a series of reflections in "Innis and Communication" by seminar participants. In November 1954, the *Explorations* researchers attended the "Institute on Culture and Communication" organised by Ray Birdwhistell at the University of Louisville's Interdisciplinary Committee on Culture and Communication. A number of the contributions to *Explorations* 3 are essays or early drafts of contributions related to this conference (Birdwhistell, Lee, Trager & Hall). The issue also includes the initial, and substantially divergent, assessments of the group's first "media experiment" at CBC studios (April 1954) in the contributions by Carpenter and Williams. The issue is rounded out with an excerpt on reading and writing (Chaytor), a new translation of Kamo Chomei's *Hojoki* (Rowe & Kerrigan), a study of utopias (Wolfenstein), a reading of *Tristram Shandy* (MacLean), reflections on Soviet ethnography (Potekin & Levin), a reading of Shelley's hallucinations as narcissism and doublegoing (McCullough), a critical reassessment of the science of human behaviour (Wallace), and "Meat Packing and Processing," an anonymous entry, likely by McLuhan, alluding to Giedion's *Mechanization Takes Command* (1948). Like *Explorations* 1, the cover depicted an indigenous mask from the Northwest Coast also represented in the Crawley film *The Loon's Necklace* (1948).

Explorations 4

According to McLuhan, *Explorations* 4 was planned as an issue devoted to Sigfried Giedion. Published in February 1955, with a cover adapted from Kandinsky's *Comets* (1938), *Explorations* 4 was devoted to issues of space and placed a strong emphasis on modes of linguistic and poetic thought across multiple media. Poems by e. e. cummings and Jorge Luis Borges mingle with essays by seminar leaders McLuhan on "Space, Time, and Poetry," Carpenter on "Eskimo Poetry: Word Magic," Tyrwhitt on "The Moving Eye" (regarding comparative perceptual experiences of Western cities and the ancient Indian city of Fatehpur Sikri), and Williams on "auditory space"—a notion that "electrified" the group, as Carpenter later recounted. Northrop Frye and Stephen Gilman's essays on poetic traditions were juxtaposed with Millar MacLure and Marjorie Adix's odes to Dylan Thomas, who had died in 1953. Case studies by then graduate students Walter J. Ong on "Space in Renaissance Symbolism" and Joan Rayfield on "Implications of English Grammar" were aligned with Dorothy Lee's contribution on "Freedom, Spontaneity and Limit in American Linguistic Usage" and Lawrence Frank's early draft of "Tactile Communication." Both Lee and Frank had presented their contributions at Ray Birdwhistell's "Institute on Culture and Communication" in Louisville, in 1954. A "Media Log" and the now famous entry "Five Sovereign Fingers Taxed the Breath," both largely replicated from McLuhan's 1954 *Counterblast* pamphlet, were published anonymously. In addition to "Our Enchanted Lives," a memorandum of instructions for television programming adapted from a Procter & Gamble memo, "The Party Line" offered a second alleged memorandum "To All TIME INC. Bureaus and Stringers." An "Idea File" containing insights on oral, written, and technological cultural forms was culled from writings by Robert Graves, Edmund Leach, Walter Gropius, and E. T. Hall, among many others. With *Explorations* 4, the group revealed its commitment to the belief that communication studies was deeply rooted in anthropological and literary-poetic traditions, but equally informed by studies of mechanisation, technology, and culture.

Explorations 5

The cover of *Explorations* 5 returned to the playfulness of issue 2: the image of the famous Minoan "Our Lady of the Sports" figurine, held at the Royal Ontario Museum (the authenticity of which has long been disputed) was set in front of the *Toronto Daily Star*'s 8 April 1954 Home Edition front page, featuring the headline "H-Bomb in Mass Production, U.S." This juxtaposition between ancient artefact, contemporary media, and technological production set the stage for the issue: starting with Daisetz Suzuki's description of "Buddhist Symbolism", the issue follows with McLuhan's famous analysis of TV and radio in Joyce's *Finnegans Wake*. Such contrasts of new media forms continue with a "Portrait of James Joyce," an excerpt of a 1950 "Third Programme" BBC documentary edited by W. R. Rodgers, and the two-page "Anna Livia Plurabelle" section of Joyce's *Finnegans Wake*, set in experimental typography designed by Harley Parker and Toronto's Cooper and Beatty Ltd. The issue further juxtaposes essays by E. R. Leach on cultural conceptions of time and Jean Piaget on time-space conceptions of the child; anthropologists Claire Holt and Joan Rayfield on interpenetrations of language and culture and Carpenter's study of Eskimo space concepts; Rhodra Métraux on differences between the novel, play, and film versions of *The Caine Mutiny*; Roy Campbell on the fusion of oral and written traditions in the writings of Nigerian author Amos Tutuola, including an excerpt of his 1954 novel *My Life in the Bush of Ghosts*, and Harcourt Brown on Pascal; economist Kenneth Boulding on information theory and Easterbrook on economic approaches to communication; and an excerpt from Daniel Lerner and David Riesman's work on the modernisation of Turkey and the Middle East. Tyrwhitt and Williams contributed reflections on the seminar's second media experiment in "The City Unseen," an analysis of students' perceptions of the environment of the then Ryerson Institute. Anonymous entries included "Colour and Communication" and a transcription of satirist Jean Shepherd's radio broadcast "Channel Cat in the Middle Distance," likely courtesy of Carpenter. The issue is rounded out with a Letters File and an Ideas File, with contributions from E. R. Leach, Patrick Geddes, and Lawrence Frank.

Explorations 6

Writing to the Explorations Group in 1954, Carpenter worried about the funds from the Ford grant that were available for publishing this issue. *Explorations* 6 was funded through the sales of issue 5 and possibly Carpenter's own funds. The cover image for this issue was a section of *The Great Wave*, by Katsushika Hokusai. According to Carpenter's letter, this issue summarizes the group's "ideas and findings," which though "not fully articulated" were "new and exciting." He saw the issue as "a full seminar statement." Indeed, the issue brings together the interdisciplinary reflections and comparative media studies that characterized the group's methodology: a brilliant essay by radical anthropologist Dorothy Lee on "Wintu thought" (Lee would ultimately publish six essays in *Explorations* and had a significant influence on the seminar) and two essays on television that were solicited to reflect upon different geographical differences that shaped the experiences of the new medium—one in the US (Chayefsky) and the other the Soviet Union (Sharoyeva, the "top man" in the USSR television system). Also included were Giedion's classic essay on cave painting; a reflection on the phonograph alongside a consideration of "print's monopoly" by C. S. Lewis; as well as essays by McLuhan on media and events; language and magic (Maritain); writing and orality (Riesman); color (Parker); the evolution of the human mind (Montagu); and the anonymous entries "Print's Monopoly" and "Feet of Clay," likely drafted by McLuhan and Carpenter, which take up conflicts between old and new media environments. This issue contains the full spectrum of the weekly seminar's research undertakings over a two-year period.

Explorations 7

Explorations 7 (1957), the only issue without a table of contents, was edited by Carpenter and McLuhan solely and, with issue 8, sponsored by the *Toronto Telegram*. Easterbrook and Tyrwhitt were away, and Williams wanted his name taken off the masthead, allegedly because of the publication of American writer Gershon Legman's infamous "Bawdy Song . . . in Fact and in Print," a history of erotic writing. McLuhan had contributed to Legman's short-lived but hugely influential magazine *Neurotica* (1948–52), so the two had a previous connection. But the tension between Williams and the editors might have also been due to their different interpretations of the CBC/Ryerson media experiments which explored media sensory biases with a group of students discussed in issue 3 by Williams in scientific terms, and here again by Carpenter in his essay "The New Languages" in cultural terms. Carpenter argues that each medium (radio, TV, print) "codifies reality differently." To accompany this opening essay, they each included anonymous entries: the essay "Classroom Without Walls," later attributed to McLuhan, explores the ubiquitous mediasphere outside educational institutions, which teachers must begin to consider as an inherent and unavoidable pedagogical experience, followed by "Songs of the Pogo," a reference to the popular comic and LP of the period, which pervaded the McLuhan home. McLuhan saw relationships between "Jazz and Modern Letters," juxtaposed with Carpenter's reflections on the acoustic character of ancient and preliterate symbols, masks, and traditions in "Eternal Life of the Dream." Dorothy Lee contributed two essays to the issue on lineal and non-lineal codifications examined in the Trobriand language with responses by Robert Graves. The focus on educational matters also included a review of Riesman's *Variety and Constraint in American Education* as well as examinations of the cultural specificity of the Soviet press, Soviet novels, and Soviet responses to Elvis Presley. The particularity of an oral and noncapitalistic culture had been an important point of comparison for the Explorations Group, especially Carpenter and McLuhan. Harley Parker designed the issue's cover.

Explorations 8

Explorations 8 (1957) is perhaps the most famous of all the issues. It was devoted to the oral—"Verbi-Voco-Visual"—and was edited primarily by McLuhan and again published by the *Toronto Telegram* and the University of Toronto. The issue was filled with visual experimentation; framed by extensive play with typography in the spirit of the Vorticists and for the first time the extensive use of "flexitype" by Harley Parker, then display designer at the ROM. Seen throughout are Parker's experiments with typography as well as color printing, the first time in the history of the journal. A photomontage from László Moholy-Nagy's *Vision in Motion* (1947) depicting a man's face with an ear juxtaposed over an eye is the frontispiece to the issue. The issue features seven essays, including one by McLuhan, that explore different aspects of oral culture—mostly concerned with a transition to a new orality. Twenty-four non-authored "Items," which include some previously published essays by McLuhan and Carpenter, appear as humorous intellectual sketches exploring topics like "Electronics as ESP," car commercials, bathroom acoustics, dictaphones, and of course wine. The final "Item," number 24, entitled "No Upside Down in Eskimo Art," reiterated McLuhan and Carpenter's core assertion that "after thousands of years of written processing of human experience, the instantaneous omnipresence of electronically processed information has hoicked us out of these age-old patterns into an auditory world."

Michael Darroch (University of Windsor)
Janine Marchessault (York University)
2016

VOLUME 6

The study presented below was made on the assumption that the language of a society is one of the symbolic systems in which the structured worldview is expressed. According to this assumption systems of kinship, ritual and other aspects of cultural symbolization and behaviour will yield, upon analysis, the same basis for conceptualization and categorization, the same approach to reality and definition of truth.

A basic tenet of the Wintu language, expressed both in nominal and verbal categories, is that reality—ultimate truth—exists irrespective of man. Man's experience actualizes this reality, but does not otherwise affect its being. Outside man's experience, this reality is unbounded, undifferentiated, timeless. Man believes it but does not know it. He refers to it in his speech but does not assert it; he leaves it untouched by his senses, inviolate. Within his experience, the reality assumes temporality and limits. As it impinges upon his consciousness he imposes temporary shape upon it. Out of the undifferentiated qualities and essences of the given reality, he individuates and particularizes, impressing himself diffidently and transiently, performing acts of will with circumspection. Matter and relationships, essence, quality are all given. The Wintu actualizes a given design, endowing it with temporality and form through his experience. But he neither creates nor changes; the design remains immutable.

The given as undifferentiated content is implicit in the nominal categories of the Wintu. Nouns—except for kinship terms, which are classified with pronouns—all make reference primarily to generic substance. To the Wintu, the given is not a series of particulars, to be classed into universals. The given is unpartitioned mass; a part of this the Wintu delimits into a particular individual. The particular then exists, not in nature, but in the consciousness of the speaker. What to us is a class, a plurality of particulars, is to him a mass or a quality or an attribute. These concepts are one for the Wintu; the word for *red*, for example, is the same as for *redness* or *red-mass*. Plurality, on the other hand, is not derived from the singular and is of slight interest to him. He has no nominal plural form, and when he does use a plural word, such as *men*, he uses a root which is completely different from the singular word; *man* is wi'Da but *men* is q'i·s.

To some one brought up in the Indo-European tradition, this is a position hard to understand. We know that the plural is derived from the singular. It is logical and natural for our grammars to start with the singular form of a noun or a verb, and then go on to the plural. When we are faced with words like group or herd or flock, we call them, as a matter of course, collective plurals. Words like sheep or deer, which make no morphological distinction between singular and plural, are explained on the basis of historical accident or the mechanics of enunciation. But to the Wintu it is natural to speak of deer or salmon without distinction of number; to him a flock is a whole, not a collection of singular individuals. To us, the distinction of number is so important that we cannot mention an object unless we also simultaneously indicate whether it is singular or plural; and if we speak of it in the present tense, the verb we use must echo this number. And the Greek had to do more than this; if he had to make a statement such as *the third man who entered was old and blind*, the words *third, who entered, was, old* and *blind*, though referring to nonquantitative concepts, all had to reiterate the singularity of the man. The Wintu, on the other hand, indicates number only if he, the speaker, chooses to do so. In such a case he can qualify his noun with a word such as *many* or *one*; or he can express plurality of object or subject through special forms of the verb.

The care which we bestow on the distinction of number, is lavished by the Wintu on the distinction between particular and generic. But here is a further difference. Whereas we find number already present in substance itself, the Wintu imposes particularity upon substance. We MUST use a plural when we are confronted by plural objects; the Wintu CHOOSES to use a particularizing form. It is true that for certain nouns, such as those referring to live people and animals, the Wintu uses a particularizing form almost always; that for substances which we, also, regard as generic, such as fire and sand and wood, he almost always uses a generic form. But these are merely habitual modes of speaking from which he can and does deviate.

His distinction, then, is subjective. He starts from *whiteness* or *white* (xayi), a quality, and derives from this, as an observer, the particular— the *white one* (xayit). With the use of derivative suffixes, he delimits a part of the mass. We take the word for *deer*, (no·B+'; the ' is the sign of the particular in the nominative), for example. In the instances I give I shall use only the objective case, no·B for the generic, and no:Bum for the particular. A hunter went out but saw no *deer*, no·B; another killed a *deer*, no·Bum. A woman carried *deer*, no·B, to her mother; a hunter brought home *deer*, no:Bum. Now the woman's deer was cut in pieces and carried, a formless mass, in her back-basket; but the man carried his two deer slung whole from his shoulder. Some brothers were about to eat venison; they called, 'Old man, come and eat *venison*, (no·B).' The old man replied, 'You can eat that stinking *venison*, (no·Bum) yourselves.' The brothers saw it just as deer-meat; to the old man it was the flesh of a particular deer, one which had been killed near human habitation, fed on human offal. I have recorded two versions of the same tale, told respectively by a man and a woman. The man refers to a man's weapons and implements in the particular; the woman mentions them all as generic. The use of the word sem (se^c) is illuminating in this connection. As sem generic, it means *hand* or *both hands* of one person, the fingers merged in one mass; spread out the hands, and now you have delimited parts of the hand, semum, *fingers*.

For the Wintu, then, essence, or quality, is generic and found in nature; it is permanent and remains unaffected by man. Form is imposed by man, through act of will. But the impress man makes is temporary. The deer stands out as an individual only at the moment of his speech; as soon as he ceases speaking, the deer merges into deerness.

The concept of the immutability of essence and the transiency of form, of the fleeting significance of delimitation, is reflected in Wintu mythology. Matter was always there; the creator, *He who is above*, a vague being, was really a Former. People do not *come into being* as I say in my faulty literal translation of the myths; they *grow out of the ground*; they always existed. Dawn and daylight, fire and obsidian have always been in existence, hoarded; they are finally stolen, and give a new role. In the myths, various characters *form* men out of materials which are already present; Coyote, for example, changes sticks into men. Throughout, form is shifting and relatively unimportant. The characters, Coyote, Buzzard, Grizzly-Bear, etc., are bewilderingly men and animals in their attributes, never assuming stable form. Even this semi-defined form may be changed with ease; Grosbeak is steamed faultily, for example, and

3

turns into a grasshopper. The Wintu speak of these characters in English as *Coyote, Loon,* not *a coyote*. We have assumed that by this they mean a proper name. But it is probable that they refer to something undelimited, as we, for example, distinguish between fire and a fire. These characters die and reappear in another myth without explanation. They become eventually the coyotes and grizzly-bears we know, but not through a process of generation. They represent a prototype, a genus, a quality which, however, is not rigidly differentiated from other qualities.

The premise of primacy of the whole finds expression in the Wintu concept of himself as originally one, not a sum of limbs or members. When I asked for a word for the body I was given the term *the whole person*. The Wintu does not say *my head aches*; he says *I head ache*. He does not say *my hands are hot*; he says *I hands am hot*. He does not say *my leg*, except extremely rarely and for good reason, such as that his leg has been severed from his body. The clothes he wears are part of this whole. A Wintu girl does not say *her dress was striped* but *she was-dress-striped*. In dealing with the whole, the various aspects referred to are generic; only when particularization is necessary as a device to distinguish toes or fingers from feet and hands is it used. But when the leg is not part of the whole, when the subject is cutting out the heart of a victim, then particularization is used, since the activity is seen from the point of view of the subject. And when a woman is ironing her dress, which is not part of her body any more, she refers to it as something separate: *my dress*.

In his verbal phrase, the Wintu shows himself again humble in the face of immutable reality, but not paralyzed into inactivity. Here again he is faced with being which is, irrespective of himself, and which he must accept without question. A limited part of this comes within his ken; his consciousness, cognition, and sensation act as a limiting and formalizing element upon the formless reality. Of this delimited part he speaks completely in terms of the bounds of his own person. He uses a stem, derived from the primary root, which means *I know,* or *this is within experience*. The definitive suffixes which he uses with this convey, in every case, the particular source of his information, or, to put it differently, the particular aspect of himself through which he has become cognizant of what he states. The material he presents has become known to him through his eyes,—'the child is playing (-be:) in the sand'; or through his other senses—'this is sour (-nte·)' or 'he is yelling (-nte·)'; or through his logic—'he is hungry (-el: he must be hungry since he has had no food for two days)'; or through the action of logic upon the circumstantial evidence of the senses—'a doe went by with two fawns (-re·: I see their tracks)'; or through his acceptance of hearsay evidence— they fought long (-ke·: someone told me).' In this category of experi-

4

ence, the future is stated in terms of intention or desire or attempt. This is a future which depends on an act of will and is not stated with certainty. This is the aspect of experience with which the unreflective among us concern themselves exclusively; as one of my students asked: 'And what is left outside?'

Outside is the reality which is beyond personal cognition, a reality which is accepted in faith. For this, the Wintu uses the primary form of the verb. Alone this stem forms a command; yoqu means *wash! you must wash*, a reference to given necessity. With the aid of different suffixes, this stem may refer to a timeless state, as when setting given conditions for a certain activity; or to what we call the passive, when the individual does not participate as a free agent. In general, it refers to the not-experienced and not-known. To this stem is appended the non-assertive -mina, and the resulting verbal form contains, then, potentially both positive and negative alternatives simultaneously. With the proper auxiliaries, this may either be used to negate, or to ask a question requiring a yes-or-no answer; or in phrases implying ignorance; but it can never assert the known. And when a Wintu gives a negative command, he uses this form again; he does not say 'don't chop' but *may it remain unactualized-chop* (k'oBmina). To this not-experienced, timeless, necessary reality, the Wintu refers chiefly in terms of natural necessity; by means of one suffix, -le's, (a nominal form of -le) he refers to a future that must be realized, to a probability which is at the same time potential, necessary and inevitable. Words modified by this suffix, are translated by the Wintu variously with the aid of *may*, or *might*, or *would*, or *must*, or *can* or *shall*. Another reference to this reality is made with the aid of the unmodified -le. This suffix can be used with personal suffixes, to indicate a future of certainty, in the realization of which the subject does not participate as a free agent. It is a future so certain, that this form, also, is sometimes translated with *must*; for example, 'You, too, shall die.' Without personal endings, the -le ties together with two events or states of being in inevitable sequence, with no reference to specific time. The sequence may be translated by the Wintu with the aid of the purposive *so as to*, or *to* or with *about to*, but there is no subjective purpose involved; or the word *before* may be used in the translation. Now the -le refers to a succession of events in nature, and to an inevitable sequence. But here the Wintu can act of his own free will and decide on one of the members of the sequence. He can interpolate an act of choice and thus bring about a desired sequence. Or the subject can intercept an undesirable sequence, by changing the first unit. The same stem is used for this, but a different suffix -ken (second person), which the Wintu translates either as *so that you should not*, or *you might* or *don't*; that is, the suffix warns of the pending sequence, and implies: avoid it. For

5

example, a man shouts to his daughter who is standing on a ladder, *Be careful, you might fall off* or *don't fall off* (talken). Some one instructs two boys: sight carefully when you shoot, *so as not to miss*, or *you might miss*, or *don't miss* (manaken). And a woman, who hears that a rattlesnake has been seen near the water, says, 'Let me not go swimming; I *might get stung* (t'optcukida).' Bia ihkedi: *he might do it himself*, or *don't let him do it*, is, according to my informant, equivalent to saying, 'you'd better do it yourself.' So the role of the Wintu in the future is not creative, but can be formative, *i.e.*, it is either negative, or takes the form of an interpolation between necessary events. Here, again the act of will exists, but appears as restrained and limited.

It is impossible to tell to what extent the reluctance to penetrate beyond external form is active in the formation of words. If the Wintu offers me an English word in translation for a Wintu one, I rarely have any way of knowing what exactly the word means to him. When he says that watca· is to *weep*, for example, is he, like me, thinking of the whole kinaesthetic activity with all its emotional implications, or is he merely concerned with the sound of weeping, as I think he is? Whenever I find a group of words derived from the same root, I can clearly see that they point to a preoccupation with form alone. I find in my glossary a word for *to shave the head* (poyoqDe·luna·), for example. There is no reason to question the English rendering till I examine the root from which it is derived. I find other derivatives from this root. One means: to *pull off a scab*; another *to have a damp forehead*. If there is to be a common meaning the first is not concerned with the activity of prying off a scab, or with the sensation of the skin; it refers only to the glistening skin exposed. Neither is the second concerned with the sensation of dampness, but, again, merely with the appearance of the skin. So, though the Wintu uses *to shave the head* as equivalent to poyoqDe·luna·, I am concerned rather with the activity of cutting itself, with the feel of the scalp, the complete removal of hair, whereas the Wintu refers only to the way the end result appears to the observer; his word means *to make one's own scalp glisten*. I have recorded a word which applies to the pounding of non-brittle objects. I have translated it as to pound to a pulp. I have passed judgment as to what happens to the consistency of the buckeye when I pound it. But the Wintu is merely making a statement as to the external form of the pounded mass; from this word *Dira·*, he derives his word for De·rus, *tick*. The same insistence upon outward form alone has influenced the naming of White traits. Where I say *he plays the piano*, the Wintu says *he makes a braying noise*. I name the automobile after its locomotion, an essential aspect of its being. But the Wintu in his pre-occupation with form alone, finds no incongruity in classifying the automobile with the turtle as: it looks like an inverted pot in motion.

6

Especially illustrative of this attitude are the words tliDiq' and -lila, which the Wintu uses in situations where we would have used *make, create, manufacture*; or, more colloquially, *fix*. But these English equivalents are far from the meaning of the Wintu words, -lila, which I have often translated as *manufacture*, actually means *to turn into, to transform*; that is, to change one form into another. And tliDiq' does not mean *make*; it means *to work on*. Our make often implies creation, the tlDiq' finds matter, assumes its presence. Make presupposes an act of aggression, the imposition of self upon matter; tliDiq' also involves an act of will but one which is restrained and spends itself on the surface.

This respect for the inviolability of the given finds further expression in the conception of the relationship between self and other. Two Wintu suffixes, which in English are rendered as coercive, reflect this attitude. One of these is -i·l or -wil, which is used to transitivize a verb, when the object is particular. For example, DiBa. means *to cross* (a river or ridge); DeBuwil means *to take across* (a child, beads, weapons, etc.) But the -i·l may also mean *to do with*; so that DeBuwil may mean *to go across with*. There is the term be·wil which means *to possess something particular*; but it also means *to be with*. The initiative is with the subject in both cases; but there is no act of aggression; there is a coordinate relationship. The word suki·l, applied to a chief, I have translated as *to rule*; but the word means *to stand with*. We would say, at best, that the suffix has the two meanings at the same time; but the Wintu makes no distinction between the two concepts, except when he has to use a language which reflects a habit of thought that regards this distinction as natural.

Another suffix which, like the -i·l, deals with the relationship of self and other, is -ma·. This sometimes appears as a causative; for example, ba· means *to eat* and ba·ma· means *to feed*, that is, *to give to eat, to make eat*. Bira· means *to swallow*; Beruma· *to fish with bait*. But like the -i·l this too implies a coordinate relationship, and one of great intimacy between self and other; for example a chief tells his people (*with the coming* of the Whites) *you shall hunger*—bira·lebo·sken, *your children shall hunger*— birama·lebo·sken (literally *children you shall hunger in respect of*). The relatives of a pubescent girl—balas—are referred to as balm·s (*they were pubescent in respect of*). A man says, koyuma· da ila:m; kuya: is *to be ill*; the man says in effect *I am ill in respect to my child*. I use *in respect to* for an other which is not entirely separated from the self, and with which the self is intimately concerned. What we express as an act of force, is here expressed in terms of continuity between self and other.

I have avoided advisedly the use of the term identification here. This term implies an original delimitation and separation. It is the nearest that

7

our social scientists, starting from delimitation, can come to unity. But if the Wintu starts with an original oneness, we must speak, not of identification, but of a premise of continuity. We find this premise underlying, not only linguistic categories, but his thought and behaviour throughout. It is basic to the Wintu attitude toward society, for example. It explains why kinship terms are classified, not with the substantives, but with the pronouns such as *this*; why the special possessives used with them, such as the neD, in neDDa·n· *my father*, are really pronouns of participation, to be used also with aspects of one's identity as, for example, my act, my intention, my future death. To us, in the words of Ralph Linton, 'society has as its foundation an aggregate of individuals.' For the Wintu, the individual is a delimited part of society; it is society that is basic, not a plurality of individuals. Again, this premise of the primacy of the unpartitioned whole gives a valid basis to beliefs such as that a man will lose his hunting luck if he goes on a hunt while his wife is menstruating. Where formal distinctions are derivative and transitory, a man is at one with his wife in a way which is difficult if not impossible for us to appreciate.

There is further the Wintu premise of a reality beyond his delimiting experience. His experience is that of a reality as shaped by his perception and conceptualization. Beyond it is the timeless design to which his experiences has given temporality. He believes in it, and he taps it through his ritual acts and his magic, seeking luck to reinforce and validate his experiential skills and knowledge, to endow his acts with effectiveness. A hunter must have both skill and luck; but skill is the more limited. An unskilled hunter who has luck, can still hit a deer by rare chance, but a skilled hunter without luck can never do so. The myths contain examples of hunters who, having lost their luck, can never kill a deer again. Now knowledge and skill are phrased agentively and experientially; but luck is phrased passively or in terms of non-actualized reality. The hunter who has lost his luck does not say *I cannot kill deer any more, but Deer don't want to die for me*. The natural, reached through luck, is impersonal; it cannot be known or sensed, and it is never addressed; but not so the supernatural. It can be felt or seen; it is personal. It is within experience. Such experience can be questioned and proof of it is often offered; the doctoring shaman produces as evidence the fish he has extracted from a patient, the missile of some supernatural being. Klutchie, a shaman, offers his knowledge of a coast language as proof that, during a protracted trance of which he has no memory, he was carried by a spirit to the West Coast. But natural necessity is beyond question, and demands no proof. It is only implied; there is no name for it. The supernatural is named and can be spoken of. Toward the supernatural the Wintu performs acts of will. The shaman, speaking to the spirit he controls, will command and demand. But the man who dives deep into a sacred pool to seek luck, will say *May it happen that I win at gambling.* His request is non-agentive and impersonal; he does not address nature, neither does he command.

Recurring through all this is the attitude of humility and respect toward reality, toward nature and society. I cannot find an adequate English term to apply to a habit of thought which is so alien to our culture. We are aggressive toward reality. We say, This is bread; we do not say like the Wintu, *I call this bread,* or *I feel* or *taste* or *see it to be bread.* The Wintu never says starkly *this is*; if he speaks of reality which is not within his own restricting experience, he does not affirm it, he only implies it. If he speaks of his experience, he does not express it as categorically true. Our attitude toward nature is coloured by a desire to control and exploit. The Wintu relationship with nature is one of intimacy and mutual courtesy. He kills a deer only when he needs it for his livelihood, and utilizes every part of it, hoofs and marrow and hide and sinew and flesh; waste is abhorrent to him, not because he believes in the intrinsic virtue of thrift, but because the deer had died for him. A man too old to fend for himself prays:

> . . . . I cannot go up to the mountains in the west to you, deer;
> I cannot kill you and bring you home . . . .
> You, water, I can never dip you up and fetch you home again . . .
> You who are wood, you wood, I cannot carry you home on my shoulder.[1]

This is not the speech of one who has plucked the fruits of nature by brute force. In conclusion, I quote an old woman, who, speaking in sorrow of the coming of the Whites, expresses the two attitudes towards nature:

> The white people never cared for land or deer or bear. When we Indians kill meat, we eat it all up. When we dig roots, we make little holes . . . We don't chop down the trees. We only use dead wood. But the white people plow up the ground, pull up the trees, kill everything. . . . The spirit of the land hates them. They blast out trees and stir it up to its depths. They saw up the trees. That hurts them. The Indians never hurt anything. . . .[2]

Dorothy Lee

[1] Dorothy Lee, 'Some Indian Texts Dealing With the Supernatural.' *The Review of Religion,* page 407, May, 1944.
[2] Cora DuBois, Wintu Ethnography, *University of California Publications in American Archaeology and Anthropology,* 36.76.
The following papers by the present author give the detailed material on which this paper is based. 'Conceptual Implications of a Primitive Language,' *Philosophy of Science,* vol. 5, 89–102, 1938; 'Some Indian Texts dealing with the Supernatural,' *The Review of Religion,* 403–411, 1941; 'Categories of the Generic and the Particular in Wintu,' *American Anthropologist,* 46.362-9. For the classification of kinship terms, see: 'Kinship Terms in Wintu Speech,' *American Anthropologist,* 42. 604-6. For words dealing with the formal rather than the kinaesthetic aspect of activity see: 'The Linguistic Aspect of Wintu Acculturation,' *American Anthropologist,* 45. 347-40. For material on the relationship between self and other: 'Notes on the Conception of the Self Among the Wintu Indians.' *The Journal of Abnormal and Social Psychology,* 45:3, 1950, reprinted in revised form in *Explorations.*

I sabotage the sentence! With me is the naked word.
I spike the verb—all parts of speech are pushed over on their backs.
I am the master of all that is half-uttered and imperfectly heard.
Return with me where I am crying out with the gorilla and the bird.
One-way Song

The Western world is living through its own past and the pasts of many forgotten cultures.

We think we are watching the rushes of recently shot film as we let the dreaming historical eye of the projector god entertain us.

Print merely permitted a fixed stereoptic vision of the past. Its imagery-flow was much greater than writing or speech permitted. But it was very far from the simultaneity that came first with the telegraph, and which now characterizes all phases of our culture.

The telegraph gave us the global snap-shot which knocked out the walls between capitals and cultures, and created 'open diplomacy', or diplomacy without walls.

Olivier's *Richard III* movie gives as a single experience the specialist knowledge of many historians of English art and society. It would take one person many years to assemble the details of the past that are there made available to the six-year-old and the professor alike. The simultaneous convergence of many kinds of specialist knowledge results in knocking out all specialist walls. It knocks out the walls between historical and biological categories equally. The child can enter the past as easily as the trained archeologist. History is abandoned to the Bridey Murphys.

We can now move into any past on the same terms at least as the cabdriver possesses the present. The upshot of the minute and exact reproduction of a phase of the English past is that it is as vulgarly familiar as the urban features of our own present.

This is not to point a moral.

The same state of affairs resulting from simultaneity of communication appears in our cities. Cities were always a means of achieving some degree of simultaneity of association and awareness among men. What the family and the tribe had done in this respect for a few, the city did for many. Our technology now removes all city walls and pretexts.

The oral and acoustic space of tribal cultures had never met a visual reconstruction of the past. All experience and all past lives were *now*. Pre-literate man knew only simultaneity. The walls between men, and between arts and sciences, were built on the written or visually arrested word.

With the return to simultaneity we enter the tribal and acoustic world once more. Globally.

As primeval man pressed on his acoustic walls and moved forward the visual orientation of experience, he discovered sculpture and painting as sculpture. Sculpture is half-way to architecture and writing.

Sculpture is not the enclosure of space. It is the modelling of space. But to a purely acoustic culture such a means of arresting visually the dynamics of acoustic space must inevitably appear as very astonishing.

Purely acoustic space, the space evoked by the spoken word in a pre-literate world, is equally magical. The complex harmonic structure of the word can never be a sign or reference before writing. It evokes the thing itself in all its particularity. Only after this acoustic magic has been enclosed in the fixed written form can it become a sign.

To capture the dynamics of the phonetic flux or flash in a fixed visual net—that was the achievement of our alphabet. This net proved to be unique. In that net the Western world took all other cultures. No other culture originally took the step of separating the sound of words from their meanings and then of translating the sound into sight.

11

This fracturing of the integrity of the word split consciousness and culture into many fragments. It transferred the rich organic compound of immemorial speech into a thin abstract cross-section which could be examined at leisure and analysed.

The analysis of visually abstracted speech brought into existence very quickly the now traditional arts and sciences and their divisions. Today, simultaneity and inclusiveness of awareness, is rapidly abolishing these divisions.

In the physical world we have the end of the age-old opposition between art and nature, as our technology reaches out to embrace light itself.

In the world of esthetics the poetic process has become the subject, plot and action of works of art. No more divisions of form and content, meaning and experience.

The new media—the new languages—which have increasingly supplemented writing and print, have begun to reassemble the multiple sensuousness of integral speech. Touch, taste, kinesthesia, sight and sound are all recreating that acoustic space which had been abolished by phonetic writing.

Under these conditions, prediction and evaluation are merely substitutes for observation. A basic feature of acoustic space is its inclusiveness. Visual space is exclusive. As our world recreates acoustic and oral culture by simply pushing on with devices of instantaneity and simultaneity, we need not fear the suppression of visual and written culture.

But the book will acquire, has already acquired, a major new role as tool of perception. It has long lost its monopoly as a channel of information. It can never lose its usefulness as a means of arresting thought and language for study. What the book was to the written manuscript, the LP disc is to music and radio.

Any change in any medium always causes modifications in all other media or languages within the same culture. Today in our simultaneous world such changes are felt as abrupt and drastic. They always were. But now we notice.

Let's now take a quick tour of the walls knocked over by media change.

Writing was the break-through from sound to sight. But with the end of the acoustic wall came chronology, tick-tock time, architecture. Writing, the enclosure of speech and sound space, split off song and dance and music from speech. It split off *harmonia* from *mimesis*.

Writing permitted the visual analysis of the dynamic logos that produced philology, logic, rhetoric, geometry, etc.

12

Modern physics and mathematics, like modern art before them, gradually abandoned visual for acoustic or non-Euclidean.

With writing on paper came the road. The road and paper meant organization at a distance: armies, empires, and the end of city walls.

But the manuscript was far from being the printed page. It was nearer to our photographic journalism. It had to be read slowly, aloud. The manuscript reader automatically found it easier to memorize all he read than refer again and again to this form. Until print, readers carried their lore at the tip of their tongues.

With print from movable type (the first application of assembly-line method to a handicraft), came fast, silent reading.

Print knocked down the monastic walls of social and corporate study. The Bible: religion without walls.

But print isolated the scholar. It created the enterprising individual who, like Marlowe's Tamburlaine or Dr. Faustus, could over-run time and history and cultures and peoples.

Print evoked the walls of the classroom.

Print could channel so much information to the individual that had previously been in the mind and memory of the teacher alone, that it upset all existing educational procedures.

It upset the monopoly of Latin by making possible multi-lingual study.

It fostered the vernaculars and enlarged the walls between nations.

It speeded up language, thereby setting new walls between speech and song, and song and instrumentation.

Print led to spoken poetry and silently read poetry, thus changing the nature of verse entirely.

Printed music entirely changed the structures of musical forms.

In America print and book-culture became the dominant form from the beginning, setting walls between literature and art, and art and life, which were less obvious in Europe.

In America print was a technological matrix of all subsequent invention. Its assembly-lines finally reached expression in Detroit and the motor-car: the home without walls.

In America the press moulded public opinion and created a new base for politics.

13

The·press was a means of mobilizing public opinion and made national road systems.

The press became in large measure a substitute for the book. But the press page is not the book page. The press creates new mental habits.

With telegraph only vernacular walls remain. All other cultural walls collapse under the impact of its instantaneous flash. With the wire-photo the vernacular walls are undermined.

The telegraph translates writing into sound. The electrification of writing was almost as big a step back towards the acoustic world as those steps since taken by telephone, radio, TV.

The telephone: speech without walls.

The phonograph: music hall without walls.

The photograph: museum without walls.

The movie and TV: classroom without walls.

Before print the community at large was the centre of education. Today, information-flow and educational impact outside the classroom is so far in excess of anything occurring inside the classroom that we must reconsider the educational process itself.

The classroom is now a place of detention, not attention. Attention is elsewhere.

It is now obvious that as all languages are mass media, so the new media are new languages. To unscramble our Babel we must teach these languages and their grammars on their own terms. This is something quite different from the educational use of audio-visual aids or of closed-circuit TV.

Marshall McLuhan

TELEVISION'S FORM OF DRAMA

If *Marty* were done on the stage, you would find that the simple throwing of a pass at a girl barely makes your first-act curtain. You would have to invent much more incisive scenes and incidents. I cannot imagine a stage play on this subject which wouldn't require a scene showing the man ending up with a rank homosexual, so that the dramatic point is made. Or else you would have to write pages of pseudopsychoanalysis in order to get the point across. The theater audience is so far away from the actual action of the drama. They cannot see the silent reactions of the players. They must be told in a loud voice what is going on. The plot movement from one scene to another must be ,marked, rather than gently shaded as is required in television. In the end, you would have a play that would interest the audience a good deal, but not to the point where they would say, 'My God, that's just like me.'

Playrights have never plumbed the subconscious levels of their characters, except perhaps in the broadest and most primitive fashion. In television, you can dig into the most humble, ordinary relationships; the relationships of bourgeois children to their mother, of middle-class husband to wife, of white-collar father to his secretary—in short, the relationships of the people.

I do not like to theorize about drama. I suspect the academic writer, the fellow who can precisely articulate his theater. However, it is my current belief that the function of the writer is to give the audience some shred of meaning to the otherwise meaningless patterns of their lives. Our lives are filled with endless moments of stimulus and depression. We relate to each other in an incredibly complicated manner. Every fiber of relationship is worth a dramatic study. There is far more exciting drama in the reasons why a man gets married than in why he murders someone. The man who is unhappy in his job, the wife who thinks of a lover, the girl who wants to get into television, your father, mother, sister, brothers, cousins, friends—all these are better subjects for drama than Iago. What makes a man ambitious? Why does a girl always try to steal her kid sister's boy friends? Why does your uncle attend his annual class reunion faithfully every year? Why do you always find it depressing to visit your father? These are the substances of good television drama; and the deeper you probe into and examine the twisted, semiformed complexes of emotional entanglements, the more exciting your writing becomes.

Paddy Chayefsky

THE ORAL AND WRITTEN TRADITIONS

I want to deal with three large questions: (1) what are the differences between cultures which depend entirely upon the spoken word and those which depend on print; (2) what will be the significance of the written word now that newer mass media have developed; and (3) what is likely to happen in those countries where the tradition of books is not fully established and where newer media are already having a decisive impact.

In the beginning the only word was the spoken word. Anthropologists no longer speak of the peoples they study as primitives, let alone savages; they prefer the less argumentative term 'preliterate' and I do not think they are wrong in making literacy the decisive dividing point. There are important differences, of course, between the preliterate tribe which depends entirely on an oral tradition and the peasant culture where illiterate folk dwell within the moral and intellectual ambit of a tradition of written literature, as in China or India. Here we may merely note that where an oral tradition is exclusive, there is a tendency for the old to have an exalted place as the storage banks of experience and entertainment, whereas writing, as in Egypt, tends to foster hierarchies of skill rather than age.

The impact of the spoken word in a preliterate culture is conveyed in the following passage from a Papago Indian woman's autobiography:

The men from all the villages met at Basket Cap Mountain, and there my father made them speeches, sitting with his arms folded and talking low as all great men do. Then they sang the war songs:

O, bitter wind, keep blowing
That therewith my enemy
Staggering forward
Shall fall.

Many, many songs they sang but I, a woman, cannot tell you all. I know that they made the enemy blind and dizzy with their singing and that they told the gopher to gnaw their arrows. And I know that they called on our dead warriors who have turned into owls and live in Apache country to come and tell them where the enemy were.

From such accounts we become aware of the emotional force that can be harnessed by the spoken or sung word in such a group—so powerful here that it can shatter the morale of a distant enemy and can bring alive the desert with its small creatures slipping like spies through the bush. On such an occasion the quiet voice of the father is resonant with the memories of the tribe. And so, too, on less formal occasions, as when on long winter nights the Papago woman's brothers would say, 'My father, tell us something', and her father, lying quietly on his mat, would slowly start to recount how the world began:

Our story about the world is full of songs, and when the neighbours heard my father singing they would open our door and step over the high threshold. Family by family they came, and we made a big fire and kept the door shut against the cold night. When my father finished a sentence we would all say the last word after him.

Implicit here is the fact that a society dependent on oral traditions and oral communications is, by our standards, a slow-paced one: there is time enough, for grown-ups as well as children, to roll back the carpet of memories.

As long as the spoken or sung word monopolizes the symbolic environment, it is particularly impressive; but once books enter that environment, it can never be quite the same again—books are, so to speak, the gunpowder of the mind. Books bring with them detachment and a critical attitude that is not possible in an oral tradition. When a society depends on memory, it employs every device of the demagogue and the poet: rhyme, rhythm, melody, structure, repetition. Since we tend to remember best things most deeply felt, the memorable words in an oral tradition are often those most charged with group feeling and those which keep alive in the individual the childhood sense of dependence, the terrors and elations of the young and something of their awe for the old. (Indeed, one can hardly speak of *individuals* in the modern sense in such cultures, since individuation depends to some degree on social differentiation and distance.) On the other hand, one thinks of the specialists on recollection in some tribes who can recall the prayers for rain and other ceremonies with word-perfect accuracy: here the individual words have lost affective tone and rote learning has taken the place of fireside forensics.

Virtually everyone in a preliterate tribe is a specialist in the oral tradition. Eggan reports that in the remote islands of the Philippines messages are conveyed orally with an accuracy fabulous to us, aware as we are that a message or rumour need only pass through two or three persons before becoming unrecognizable. For these tribesmen, words are like buckets in a fire-brigade, to be handled with full attention, while we feel we can afford to be careless with the spoken word, backstopped as we are by the written one.

Of course, in another sense we all began life as preliterates; our written tradition is backstopped by an oral one. Adult culture—which is largely the culture of the written word—blots out for most of us our childhood imagery; this gets lost, not, as Freud thought, because it is sexual and forbidden, but because it is irrelevant to us as literate people. We still dream in this earlier, 'forgotten language', and our great artists often renew themselves and us by translations from this language into the written vernacular of the adult.

The proverb, as an invented repository of tribal lore and wisdom, is a bridge between the oral and the written stages of history. Edwin Loeb writes that the proverb, as a kind of abstract, generalizing, easily remembered statement about experience—the most literate, so to speak, of the preliterate styles of speech—is associated only with cattle-raising people. It is among such relatively advanced, semi-nomadic people that the need for a distinct body of property laws first tends to be felt—who does the new calf belong to?—and the proverb is a convenient mnemonic of tribal judgments. Many of our earliest sacred writings are collections of proverbs.

The late Harold A. Innis took a rather crabbed, Spenglerian pleasure in showing that the materials on which words were written have often counted for more than the words themselves. For instance, he argues that papyrus, being light and readily stored in a desert land, put the priests of Egypt in command of the calendar and, in Big Brother fashion, of social memory, and was essential to the spread of the Egyptian dynasties in space and the hegemony of the priests in time. The clay tablets of Sumeria were put out of business by the greater convenience of the newer forms, just as many downtown movie houses have been put out of business by TV and the drive-ins. Perhaps it was understandable that a Canadian should be one of the first to study such problems systematically, after watching his country's forests being cut down on behalf of the *Reader's Digest* and other forms of American pulpular imperialism.

The book is one of the first, and very possibly the most important, mass produced product, and its impact demonstrates the falsity of the common notion that mass production *per se* brings about the massification of men. Print, in replacing the illuminated manuscript, created the silent, compulsive reader, his head bobbing back and forth across the lines like a shuttle, working in a monotone of colour and a metronome of motion—a semi-automatic scanner. This in contrast with the colour and variety of 'reading' an illuminated manuscript, where reading was ordinarily aloud, in a group, and where the illustrations enlivened the occasion, made it more sensuous and less rationalistic. Such reading appears in historical perspective as a transitional stage between the spoken and the silent word, while movies and TV have brought back some of the qualities and emotional states associated with the manuscript era.

The book, like the door, is an encouragement to isolation: the reader wants to be alone, away from the noise of others. This is true even of comic-books for children who associate comics with being alone, just as they associate TV with the family, and movies with friends of their own age.

Thus the book helps liberate the reader from his group and its emotions, and allows the contemplation of alternative responses and the trying on of new emotions. Weber has stressed the importance of the merchant's account book in rationalizing the merchant and his commerce; other historians have made familiar the role of the printed Bible in challenging the authority of the Roman Church. Luther, and especially Calvin, increasing by their doctrine the growing isolation of men, invited each pilgrim to progress by himself, Book in hand, while at the same time trying to institute a new authority in place of the old. But, as the dissident sects of Protestantism illustrate, the book tends to be a solvent of authority: just as there are still blank pages in the merchant's account book waiting to be filled, so there is always the question, when one has challenged traditional authority, 'What next?'

At the same time, while the book helped people break away from family and parish, it linked them into non-contiguous associations of true believers. The Polish peasant who learned to read and write became identified with the urban world of progress and enlightenment, of ideology and utopia, even while still in the peasant world. This identification had many of the elements of a conversion, print itself and the world it opened up being a kind of gospel. In this country of near-universal literacy we have forgotten the enthusiasm for print which can burst on people newly literate—the 'each one, teach one' movements of Mexico, the Philippines and elsewhere, the voracity for books (for what most librarians would define as 'good' books) in the Soviet Union and other recently industrializing lands. It is no accident that self-taught industrialists like Carnegie became the promoters and patrons of the library movement in America. Among the highly educated, and in countries of long-established literacy, there is little comparable enthusiasm.

Print may be said to mark the epoch of the rise and influence of the middle class—the time-attentive, the future-oriented, the mobile. Reading and education were the highroads this class made use of to rise in the world and to move about in it during the great colonizing periods. Even the novel, denounced as frivolous and sensuous by the Puritans, had an important function in the changing society. I think not so much of its use as a device for reform and civic adult education, as in *Oliver Twist* or *Uncle Tom's Cabin*, as of its less obvious use as a device by which people might prepare themselves for novel contacts and novel life-situations—anticipatory socialization, that is, a preparation in imagination for playing roles that might emerge in one's later career. The very conception of life implicit in the notion of a career is facilitated by the dramatic structure of the novel, especially the *Bildungsroman*, with its protagonist, its interest in motive, its demand on the reader that he project himself into the experiences portrayed. In a society depending on oral tradition, individuals have life-cycles—they live through childhood; they are initiated; they are adult; they grow old; they die—but they do not have careers in our abstract sense of the term. The novel of the 19th century doubtless disoriented many chambermaids and a few duchesses, but on many more occasions it helped prepare individuals for their careers in a disorienting world of rapid industrialization and urbanization—where fictional moves and actual ones were not so unlike, and life and art could almost imitate one another.

If oral communication keeps people together, print is the isolating medium *par excellence*. People who would simply have been deviants in a preliterate tribe, misunderstanding and misunderstood, can through books establish a wider identity—can understand and even undermine the enemies of home and hearth and herd. While the geographic migrations of preliterate peoples have something in common with the incomprehending movements of herds of deer, the readers of the age of discovery were prepared mentally for some of the experiences of their geographic mobility; they had at any rate left home in imagination even if they had not roamed as far or among as strange people as they were actually to meet. The bookish education of these inner-directed men helped harden them for voyages: they wanted to convert the heathen, civilize him, trade with him—if anyone changed in the encounter, it would be the heathen, while they, as they moved about the globe or up the social ladder, remained very much the same men. The epitome of this was the Englishman in the tropics who, all alone, dressed for dinner with home guard ceremonial, toasted the Queen, and, six months late, read with a proper sense of outrage the leader in the London *Times*. His ties with the world of print helped steady him in his course far from home and alone.

Today the successors of these men are often other-directed; they are men molded as much by the mass media outside their education as by their schooling; men who are more public relations-minded than ambitious; men softened for encounters rather than hardened for voyages; if they move about the globe it is often to win the love of the natives or to try to understand their mores, rather than to exploit them for gain or the glory of God. Meanwhile the natives themselves are on the move, and the sharp differences between societies dependent on the oral tradition and those dependent on print are tending to be less important with the coming of radio and film. Often the decisive difference is among the peasants themselves within a country, such as India or the Middle East or Africa—the difference between those who listen to the radio and go to movies and those who shut these things out as the voice of the Devil or as simply irrelevant for them. In the Middle East it was found that those peasants who listened to Radio Ankara or the BBC or the VOA already had, or soon acquired, a different sensibility from those who did not. The former were prepared in the imagination for more voyages than they were likely ever to make. When these peasants were asked what they would do if they were to become President of Turkey, for example, or where they would like to live if they could not live in their native villages, they could answer the questions; they had a stock of opinions—public opinions—on such matters. But the tradition-directed peasants who were not radio listeners or movie goers could not answer the questions; to the question about becoming President they might say: '. . . How can you ask such a thing? How can I . . . President of Turkey . . . master of the whole world!' The very thought appeared sacrilegious. Nor could such people imagine living anywhere else, and when pressed some said they would die if forced to leave their village.

It is too soon to say whether the epoch of print will be utterly elided in the underdeveloped countries, just as, with the coming of electrical and atomic energy, they may skip the stage of coal and water power. Conceivably, the movies and broadcasting may awaken a hunger for print when their own novelty is worn off and they come to be used as tie-ins with print. Just as the barbarians of Europe in the Middle Ages pulled themselves up by Greek bootstraps, so the nonindustrial countries can for a long time draw on the storehouse of Western science and technology, including the science of social organization; and there are still enough inner-directed men in our society who are willing to go out and help build the armies of Iran and the factories of Istanbul.

David Riesman

High-fidelity reproduction depended for its success on high-fidelity records, and high-fidelity records in turn depended on the existence of tape recording. Tape's invasion of the recording studio, begun early in 1949, proceeded so implacably that within a year the old method of direct recording on wax or acetate blanks was almost completely superseded. Compared to the old method, tape was enticingly cheap. For an investment of a few thousand dollars one could buy a first-class tape-recorder, take it to Europe (where musicians were plentiful and low-salaried), and record great amounts of music; one could then bring the tapes back to America and have the 'custom record' department of either Columbia or RCA transfer them—at a reasonable fee—to micro-groove records.

One not only could, one did. Between August, 1949, and August, 1954, the number of companies in America publishing LP recordings increased from eleven to almost two hundred. One of them, perhaps the most successful, was the Westminster Recording Company, formed in 1949 by three phonograph enthusiasts with a capital of $23,000, which in five years had built up a catalogue of five hundred LP records and was nearing the $2-million mark in annual sales, primarily of classical music.

At the start, Westminster and its rival contemporaries had to reckon with one serious delimiting reality: the large, well-established companies had cornered the supply of famous performers and mined the lode of standard repertoire with pre-emptive thoroughness. Because of this, the post-1949 newcomers concentrated their efforts on nonstandard literature performed by nonfamous musicians. In so doing they were extraordinarily successful, artistically and commercially. The ensuing LP steeplechase left everyone breathless. From 1950 to the present, new recordings of classical music have been thrown on the market at an unheard-of tempo—more than ten thousand of them, in fact. In addition, the scramble for fresh repertoire has unearthed music long forgotten and has afforded contemporary composers a hearing they might otherwise never have enjoyed in their lifetimes.

The bounty was not falling on unreceptive ears. At the close of 1954, Toscanini's two-year-old recording of the Beethoven Ninth Symphony had found 130,331 buyers and gave no evidence of losing its sales momentum. Twenty years earlier, a recording of the Ninth Symphony did well to sell five hundred copies within a similar period; forty years earlier, a recording of the Ninth had not even been made.

Jacques Barzun commented on the unparalled musical riches of the mid-twentieth century: 'This mechanical civilization of ours has performed a miracle for which I cannot be too grateful: it has, by mechanical means, brought back to life the whole repertory of Western music—not to speak of acquainting us with the musics of the East. Formerly, a fashion would bury the whole musical past except a few dozen works arbitrarily selected. Today neglected or lesser composers come into their own and keep their place. In short the whole literature of one of the arts has sprung into being—it is like the Renaissance rediscovering the ancient classics and holding them fast by means of the printing press. It marks an epoch in Western intellectual history.'

Roland Gelatt

Américo Castro's *The Structure of Spanish History* is a study of history; yet it draws much of its 'evidence' from literature: it becomes, then, a work of criticism whose end is first a conception of Spanish history and second of the possibility of history itself.

The first Spanish edition was criticized by many historians for this attention to literature. Chapters on the *Poema del Cid* and on *Libro de buen amor*, on such versifiers of saintly biography as Gonzalo de Berceo, seemed frivolous to historians preoccupied with trade routes, military strategy, and dynastic scandal. They asked, in effect, what have works of imagination, works which at best furnish tangential information as to mediaeval customs and manners, to do with the serious setting forth of 'historical facts'?

This is an old story. A defence of Castro against the state of mind sometimes called positivism, but more accurately called 'reductionism', is unnecessary. The problem is not to justify the literary contribution to historical understanding, nor to justify the historical contribution to literary understanding; it is to comprehend how the two modes of understanding, together, become one.

Recent influential English and American critics also seek to articulate the study of literature with the study of history, but in ways different from Castro's. There is the popularity among us of 'the history of ideas'. If our orientation is toward philosophy, we have tended to follow Lovejoy's lead. If our orientation is toward literature, we have tended toward Trilling's lead to see how our culture's abstract ideas are tested, explored, destroyed or found trustworthy in literature which charges them with life. Others seek the life-source of literature in myth and the history of culture in the history of myth. Each offers us a way of having our literature now and knowing it historically too, and so through literature, of knowing ourselves in history and history in ourselves. Here, too, lies the significance of *The Structure of Spanish History*:

History is, first and foremost, a mesh of interconnected values, into which the existence of a people is articulated, whilst the people manifest their reality by accomplishing valuable actions that have actual extension in time and space.

It does not matter that we cannot agree upon the nature and form of these values and that, consequently, we cannot render them acceptable to everyone. It is enough if the historian have faith and belief in the faith that a people have objectified in their life, a faith justified in great achievements that stand for all to see, or even in a profound fear of being unable to realize great achievements. . . .

History is where are realized, in many ways, man's possibilities for achieving great deeds and works which endure and radiate their values afield. . . .

History can become universal; it does not, however, attain universality through the unifications of the peoples who are engaged in creating history, but rather by virtue of the fact that values can be universalized, can spread, near or far, from people to people. . . .

It is necessary, then, to presuppose that some kind of important value exists, before one can set about describing and trying to understand the process of history in a human collectivity, which at first glance is a confused chaos of fragments of life that in themselves are *not yet history.*

This doctrine is unhesitating, and among its numberless consequences and corollaries is that literature, and artistic creation in general, are of primary relevance to historical understanding. Since art is an expression of values, Castro's axiological approach to history depends more upon it and those things which resemble it—national myths, expressive linguistic innovations, ethical attitudes, etc.—than upon political or economic facts. In other words, Castro approaches cultural history, not with the intention of writing a history of culture, but with the belief that history *is* culture in the humanistic sense of that word. And the unavoidable consequence is that great works of literature are no longer accessory to historical

27

research. An epic poem does not just give information about an heroic age and its inhabitants. Rather, it expresses the specific quality of such an age at its greatest moments: it grants us direct insight into the sense of the age's heroism.

This approximation of history to culture brings Castro's work closer to that done by anthropologically oriented students of the 'science of man'. Among them *The Structure of Spanish History* has its best chance of finding readers equipped not only to read and judge but to make use of it. Yet Castro is no anthropologist; he is a humanist, not a social scientist. The key difference is to be found in the terms 'culture' and 'values' which he understands humanistically: he sees them from the inside out, not the outside in. He doesn't begin with observation of facts but with what is called 'intuition' and what used to be called 'appreciation'. Or to use an even older and truer word about man's relation to values, Castro 'loves' before he observes.

As the centre and subject-agent of this history, I have taken the whole workshop in which history has been fashioning itself, and not fragmentary psychological traits, always generic and meaningless in their isolation. Nor have I considered external circumstances as separable from the very course of life itself, as if the latter were given a substantial 'reality' on which causes and motives act. My idea is that a Frenchman, or a Spaniard, handles the circumstance about him according to the possibilities of his peculiar structure of life. Historical life consists in an inner trajectory or process in which the external motivations acquire form and reality; that is, they are converted into deeds and events that have a meaning.

These deeds and events trace out the peculiar physiognomy of a people and make evident the 'inwardness' of their life, never identical with that of any other human community.

A later sentence concludes this thought: 'History is understood if we contemplate it creating itself from within its peculiar mode of behaviour, and not from without.' The meaning is plain. For Castro, the terms 'culture', 'age', or 'system of values' are merely ways of designating the results of the encounter of consciousness—collective or individual—with the surrounding world. They are only words and have not (as they are likely to have for social scientists) any sort of autonomous existence. They do not cause, define conclusively, or denote, and, as a result, they cannot be observed, collected, and definitively interpreted. They must rather be understood by a kind of intuition or appreciation of the process of consciousness which is responsible for them. Thus, what Castro calls 'a people' is collectivity of awareness which acts as an artist continually creating that 'work of art' which is its history, its culture, and its values. Consequently, for him the greatest historical achievements of a people

28

are artistic in the broadest sense of that word. It is the assumption of his book, then, that the historian *is* a critic by the very nature of the things he studies.

Thus, Castro practices a new version of 'existential historicism'. He substitutes the immediacy of the creative consciousness for the abstractions of 'Geist', 'culture', or 'environmental influence' and establishes it as the foundation, the rock upon which the past must be reconstructed. But, it will be objected, how can consciousness, by definition so elusive and changeable, be a 'rock' for even the flimsiest structure of history? The point is this: by its very nature consciousness knows itself to be free, indetermined and indeterminable if it chooses to be so. Actually, consciousness may or may not be as completely governed from outside itself, as Freud once claimed it to be in a well-known lecture to Viennese medical students. But it is not Freud's opinion that counts here: it is the patent indignation and surprise of the medical students (as made evident in the words of the lecture itself). Because they felt and we feel that 'inwardness' is free at any given moment, history and consciousness seem mutually irrelevant. It is a question of tangential definitions. History, by definition, if not a chain of cause and effect, is, at least, an established relationship of some sort—an ordered sequence of past time. Consciousness, on the other hand, is a phenomenon of the present, of freedom *now* to choose the path of the future. Hence it would seem impossible to use consciousness to understand that order of concluded choices which men call history. It would seem in the deepest sense impossible to achieve Castro's major purpose: the full return of history to man.

To meet such objections, Castro—with a relentlessness characteristic of all his thought—demands specific meaning from the term 'inwardness'. He is unsatisfied with the paradoxical self-sufficiency of formulae such as Ortega F. Gasset's 'historical reason'. For Castro isn't talking about the purified, abstracted, almost theoretical consciousness of a Descartes —the reason aware of its own ability to reason. Nor is he talking about an Hegelian Absolute. Rather, he means value-creating consciousness, consciousness in significant contact with the outside world. It is the 'I' saying to itself: this is important; this is beautiful; this is mysterious. And when it says these things, while still free, it is necessarily guided, either positively or negatively, by a tradition and a social group from which it receives, or to which it proposes, its values. So much is evident; so much anthropologists will grant. But what about the problem of freedom and determination in the historical or value-creating consciousness—the problem of Boethius, and of the Viennese medical students? It's here Castro makes one of his major theoretical contributions:

This 'inwardness' is not a static and finished reality analogous to the classical substance; it is a dynamic reality. . . . But 'inwardness' is an ambiguous term. It may designate *the fact of living* within certain vital possibilities (preferences) and impossibilities (reluctances), and in this case I shall call it the 'dwelling place' of life (morada); or it may designate *the mode according to which* men live within this dwelling-place, and then I shall call it 'living structure', or 'living functioning' (vividura). Both the dwelling place and the living structure of a community of people are made manifest in the way the community speaks, thinks, believes, and makes or does for itself certain things in preference to others.

Such sentences as these depend on the whole of Castro's book for their full understanding. But a paraphrase can be attempted after reading a few other passages:

The confusion created by the aforementioned criticism [of certain German studies of national character] grows, I think, out of not saying more precisely what we mean when uttering the word 'permanent' (dauerhaft) with reference to what we call French, Spanish, etc. If it is applied to an essence, to contents with a fixed stability, of a biological racial type, substantial in some way or other, then we err, because the objectifiable content of human activities is unforeseeable—the intelligence or the stupidity, the goodness or badness, the heroism, the fainthearted-ness, the baseness of an action. For life does not consist solely in doing this or that (including doing *nothing*). . . . Life presupposes, in addition, a perfection from the historical 'dwelling' in which man finds himself placed.

There is a latent continuity in the way in which a man is stationed in his language, in his customs, and in his estimations. Stability is to variability as the stem of a verb to its conjugated forms. Thus, however unexpected may be the *what* in the history of a people, their *how* presents a structural meaning that serves as a functional link.

Castro thus believes that conscious life is free at any given moment of time to 'project' and 'construct' a valuable biography or history and that —this freedom not withstanding—the biography of history will conform to the form of its social or cultural situation. In a sense, he has reconstituted for historical purposes Bergson's evolutionary solution to the problem of freedom and determination—of free growth of life *from* hereditary and environmental possibilities. The terminology is particularly signifi-cant; for received 'culture' Castro substitutes the inward 'living structure' —the mode of choosing freely which characterizes a people's value-creation.

It is, then, the historian's task to grasp intuitively both concepts or phases of this historical consciousness. He must describe the architecture of the dwelling place, and he must return in successive flashes of insight to the monuments of self-expression and created value of a people. He must be able to communicate the mode, the quality of conscious encounter with the world, which each exemplifies in its own way. Only thus can he reveal the 'living structure' of aspiration and expression of that aspiration which is the most important thing about history—far more important than battles won or lost and wealth gained or squandered. The *Poema del Cid*, a 12th century epic devoted to the celebration of heroism, is quite unlike the *Libro de buen amor*, a tolerant, mockingly autobiographical, and immensely funny panorama of mediaeval existence as lived by a mundane priest. The 10th century myth of Santiago (a myth of divine help at moments of national crisis) in no way resembles the 17th century belief in honour (a myth of the self-sufficient personality). But the historian who has understood Spain as a dwelling place from which these differing works of literature and belief have been 'projected' historically can go on to appreciate their 'structural' similarities: he can intuit the Spanish quality of their value-creation.

There are possible objections to Castro's view, of course—for example, the undeniable modifications which ages and generations make upon the dwelling place. The concepts of a 'Middle Ages' and a 'Renaissance' still have not been stripped of meaning. And there are the difficulties of re-working Castro's thought to fit the situation of 'pre-historic' societies or even such peoples as the 'English', whose propensity to historical change seems to have been greater than that of the Spaniards. We might say, extrapolating from Castro, that we are more susceptible to history as a 'people', and, if that is the case, we must ask how are we to intuit a comprehensible dwelling place for our culture? It is enough, here, to suggest that the book is one which makes it possible to ask these questions in this way.

One result of Castro's daring is that he can relate history to literature without subjecting one to the other and without distorting either or both. He does not extract historical data from works of literature not designed for that purpose; he does not demand from historical periods and events explanations of literature. Instead he joins them where they must be joined: as living structures of conscious existence. He joins them in the place where values are made.

From his point of view, the greatest work is the most significant historically, because it is precisely this greatness that history can be interpreted as conspiring to produce. For him, that is what history is for. Cervantes can reveal more about the condition of being Spanish and of living in the 17th century, than all the minor novelists who came after him and whose works are generally used as a hunting ground for customs

and tastes. He can do it because his personal greatness creates an awareness of possibilities of his 'dwelling place'. Thus and only thus, can he
make a new 'universalized' expression of the Spanish 'living structure'.

Castro returns history to her place among the muses. He asserts in a new
way the great classical belief in the primacy of values over facts. His
work is at once an example of and a model for the history which he
would write. *The Structure of Spanish History* is, by virtue of being
major criticism, major history. In this fact lies, for those who would
understand Spain, its greatness. And in this fact too lies, for those who
strive for the understanding of other cultures, its wisdom.

3

Stephan Gilman and Roy Harvey Pearce

Foreword

'Space conception in prehistoric art' forms one of the most important chapters in my forthcoming study on *The Continuity of the Human Spirit*. Today this problem is everywhere under discussion, and scholars ask themselves for example, 'What things have changed and what have remained unchanged in human nature throughout the course of human history? What is it that separates us from other periods? What is it that, after having been suppressed and driven into the unconscious for long periods of time, is now reappearing in the imagination of contemporary artist?'

This question of the continuity of human experience has interested me deeply for several years, especially in connection with the earliest beginnings of art (in prehistory) and of architecture (in Egypt and Sumer). I soon discovered that the existing photographic reproductions of primeval art were quite insufficient for the demands of modern art history. I therefore made several visits myself to the caverns in France and Spain, at first accompanied by Hugo P. Herdeg, one of the best Swiss photographers, then with both him and Achille Weider, then, since Herdeg's untimely death two years ago, with Weider alone. Together we accumulated the necessary photographs, which of course I selected carefully so that they should bring out those aspects that I consider relate to our immediate problems. Anyone who has ever attempted to work for eight or nine hours a day in these caverns will understand the difficulties we experienced in taking these pictures, which included some that had, up till then, proved impossible to photograph.

I feel most grateful to these photographers, as also to the Rockefeller Foundation which made the whole undertaking possible.

However, I was not just hunting for photographs. I was, above all, striving to come to a closer understanding of that fundamental human experience which goes by the name 'art'.

I have no doubt that this chapter on 'space conception in prehistoric art' will meet with opposition, for it is in direct contrast to the prevailing view that in prehistory 'the single form is simply set off against chaos'.

It is my belief that art cannot exist without a relation to the space around it—a space conception. The work of contemporary artists—for example the structure of some of the works of Kandinsky and Klee—have shown us that prehistoric art is not necessarily chaotic. The art historian humbly accepts their silent lesson.

Prehistory is the pre-architectonic state of human development. As soon as architecture was evolved in Egypt and Sumer, and became pre-dominant over sculptures and paintings, a new space conception was developed, which, with many variations, existed until the building of the Pantheon in Rome. From that time on a new phase came about—another space conception—which lasted until the 19th century. A third architectural space conception set in around the turn of the 20th century.

Intangibility of Space
It is possible to give physical limits to space but, by its nature space is limitless and intangible. Space dissolves in darkness and evaporates in infinity.

Means are necessary for space to become visible: it must acquire form and boundaries either from nature or by the hand of man. All else is relative to this. Space is intangible, yet space can be perceived.

What constitutes this perception of space?

To confine emptiness within such dimensions that a form is created which elicits an immediate emotional response requires a complex set of conditions. The elucidation of the process by which an impression of inarticulate words is transformed into an emotional experience moves far away from logical reasoning.

What is it that happens?

34

In the realm of architecture, space is experienced by means of observation, in which the senses of sight and touch are interlocked. In the first instance this is a simple statement of fact. But through the relations of the most diverse elements and the degree of their emphasis—straight or curving lines, planes, structures, massivity proportions forms of all kinds —a matter of simple physical observation can be transposed to another sphere. These diverse elements are seen suddenly as a single entity, as a oneness, imbued with spiritual qualities. This transformation of a simple physical fact into an emotional experience derives from a higher level of our faculty of abstraction. Before discussing this it is necessary to go briefly into the beginnings of the perception of space and its early supremacy.

Priority of the Sense of Space

It becomes ever more evident that a comprehension of space is developed earlier than a sense of time. It is just this supremacy of the sense of space which appears with such surprising strength in the perception of prehistoric man. It was then—when there was no realization of time in its later meaning—that the sense of space developed most highly. The struggle for survival took care of this. The unerring outlines of the engraving bear witness to it. There the forms and movements of animals appear as they had been burnt into man's consciousness.

The Geneva psychologist, Jean Piaget, has established that the sense of time in children only develops indirectly.[1] To arrive at this he investigated the many stages of consciousness of the growing child. In doing this, like Levy-Bruhl in his investigations of the mentality of primitive people, Piaget started off by considering the child as an independently existing phenomena and not by approaching him from the standpoint of the adult. The sense of time is brought home to the child through his comparison of the speed at which objects move through space.

Right from the start an appreciation exists of bodily speed of movement through space, and this can be expressed in the psychological formula $c = \frac{s}{t}$: velocity $= \frac{time}{space}$. Piaget distinguishes two aspects of the sense of time: the sequence of events (before, after, at the same time), and the duration of events (longer or shorter duration). From a number of different expressions used by children aged 6–7, it appears that the sense of time developed only very gradually.

Similar observations were made by Levy-Bruhl in studying the speech of primitive peoples. In his *Mentalité Primitive* (Paris, 1922, p. 520) he says 'The conception of time, particularly in a qualitative sense,

---

[1] Jean Piaget. *Le development de la notion du temps chez l'enfant.* Neuchâtel and Paris.

remains vague. Almost all primitive speech is as poor in possibilities of expressing time relationships as it is rich in expressions of space relationships.' And, in explanation, he adds: 'Frequently a future event, especially if it has something to do with the emotions, is described in the present tense.' Beforehand, afterwards and at the same time are often difficult to distinguish from one another; today, tomorrow and yesterday are similarly interwoven. It is all an eternal present.

The Nature of Space Conception

The first observable fact about space is its emptiness, an emptiness through which things move or in which things stand. The human demiurge—the almost god-like human compulsion to invent new things and to give a spiritual quality to impressions of the senses—also operates in connection with space. Man takes cognisance of the emptiness that girdles him around and gives it a psychic form and expression.

The effect of this transfiguration which lifts space into the realm of the emotions is termed space conception. This space conception portrays man's relations with his environment.

Space conception is a psychic recording of the realities which confront him. The world which lies about him becomes transformed. He thus realises, so to speak, his urge to come to terms with it, to give a graphic expression of his position towards it.

In their first Manifesto of 1924, the Surrealists speak of an '*Automatisme psychique pur* par lequel on se propose d'exprimer, soit verbalement, soit par écrit, soit de toute autre manière, le fonctionnement réel de la pensée. Dictée de la pensée, on l'absence de toute contrôle exercé par la raison.'[1] A space conception is just such an automatic physic recording in the realm of the visible environment. It develops instinctively, usually remaining unknown to its authors. It is just because of its unconscious and, so to speak, compulsive manifestation, that a space conception provides such an insight into the attitude of a period to the cosmos, to man and to eternal values.

This attitude towards space changes continuously, sometimes by small degrees, sometimes basically. As will appear later, there have been very few space conceptions in the whole development of man. Each covered long periods of time. Within each of these epochs, however, many variations and transitions have been built up; for relations with space are always in a state of suspension, and the transitions flow in and out of one another.

---

1 André Breton, *Manifeste de Surréalisme*. Paris 1924 p. 42.

Was There a Space Conception in Prehistory?
This is a very controversial question and by no means as disassociated from the origins of art as might appear at first sight.

There are two opinions. One is admittedly dominant and has been held by generations of scholars. This view holds that the primeval art is without any kind of composition. It is uncontrolled, arbitrary and chaotic.

Moritz Hoernes (1852–1917), who as early as 1898 made a survey of all the then known examples of primeval art in Europe,[1] stated that it 'gives the impression of an orderless and directional multiplicity, an undisciplined freedom which could not achieve results because it lacked the firm tradition and assuredness afforded by the strict observance of principles of style'.[2]

The prehistoric artists do not appear 'to see any necessity whatsoever of placing their otherwise correctly executed animals in the position which we alone consider admissable, namely with their legs extending downwards and their backs up. . . . In the great melée of animals at Altamira, the baseline upon which each animal theoretically stands often deviated by 45° to 90° from the horizontal.[3]

Paleolithic art lacks 'all order and control and is without any talent for combination and composition'.[4]

This attitude has been maintained, with some shades of difference, by the prehistorians up to the present day, and has also been adopted by the archaeologists. 'There is in fact no relation whatever between form and background; the single form is simply set off against chaos.'[5] Herbert Read also finds that order and composition does not exist in Magdalenian art, and that it makes its first appearance in the axial-geometric designs of the Neolithic period.[6]

This view is opposed by only a few solitary voices. One of these, Max Raphael, in his book *Prehistoric Cave Paintings*[7] makes an analysis of the proportions of the various animals which occur in primeval art, particularly using the concave-convex outline of their backs. He finds that 'These proportions—largely independent of the various animal species represented—can be reduced to a few recurrent types, such as 1:1, 1:2, 2:3, 2:5, 3:5, 3:4, 3:7, 4:7.'[8] The first two of these do not require any

[1] Moritz Hoernes & Oswald Menghin, *Urgeschichte der bildenden Kunst in Europe*. (Vienna, 1925).
[2] *Ib.*, p. 176.
[3] *Ib.*, p. 124/25.
[4] *Ib.*, p. 194.
[5] H. A. Groenewegen-Frankfort: *Arrest & Movement* (London 1951). p. 15.
[6] *Arrest & Movement*, which deals with the basis of Egyptian and Mesopotamian art.
[7] Max Raphael *Prehistoric Cave Paintings* (New York, first printing 1945, second printing 1946.)
[8] *Ib.*, p. 28ff.

explanation as they can easily occur anywhere. The following three form that homogenous group (2:3, 2:5, 3:5) which is known as the 'golden section'. This second and more astonishing surprise will of course be met with general scepticism. In both our aesthetic and our historic thinking cave dwellers and the golden section appear absolutely incompatible. There is no need to detail here how Raphael in his explanation starts by connecting the proportions of the human hand with the golden section and with the magical implications attributed to it.[1]

Raphael goes even further in his final chapter 'The Composition of the Magic Battle of Altamira' in which he interprets the frescoes on the ceiling of this famous cavern as a conscious composition. He sees, as the two chief combatants, the gigantic light yellow hind (220 cms high) and the very powerfully emphasized black bison who stands upon a blood red magic sign. The isolated positions of the hind and the bison and their juxtaposition is undoubtedly striking. This does not however imply that one need accept any of the various explanations of their meaning (such as that the animals represent the totems of two rival clans). What matters is that Max Raphael has had the courage to see, in this dramatic ceiling of prehistoric days, definite proportions and inherent elements of composition, and by no means an orderless chaos.

Max Raphael is able to reveal such relationships because he knows well that at that time 'an axis to balance the left and right was not introduced'. Perhaps it is the absence of such an axis that leads many to believe that the picture has no composition: for under the pressure of both the Renaissance and ancient art we see in every composition an attempt to 'set right', in accordance with the rules of balance around an axis, a world that is 'out of joint'.[2]

In primeval art an unerring certainty of line and form is inextricably bound up with magical significance. It is almost impossible to comprehend this by reason alone. Only very gradually and indirectly can one begin to discern the space conception of primeval art.

The Space Conception of Primeval Art
What is the space conception of primeval art?

If by space conception we mean the power of any period to transform a simple act of perception into an emotional experience then we can say that no art exists that is not based on a relationship with space.

The space conception of a period is the graphic projection of its attitude towards the world. This holds true whether we consider the Renaissance, when everything was dominated by the eye of the beholder, which was

---

1 *Ib.*, p. 28/29.
2 *Ib.*, p. 45.

graphically depicted by perspective projection of long level vistas upon a plane surface; or Egyptian art where several different aspects of the same object are depicted upon horizontal and vertical planes undistorted and in their natural size; or again in the Neolithic period when geometric abstractions are left hovering in space.

At the base of the first two of these space conceptions lies a sense of order that has been rooted deep in our human nature for over 5000 years. This sense of order involves—at least ever since the times of Egypt and Sumer—the relation of everything that one sees to the vertical or the horizontal. Each of us carries in his brain a sort of secret balance that unconsciously impels us to weigh everything we see in relation to the horizontal and vertical. This ranges from the composition of a painting to the most ordinary of our everyday habits. We feel slightly uneasy when our knife and fork are not laid straight beside our plate at table, or when the writing paper on our desk is not parallel to the blotter. However this is not the only conception of order that can exist. There is another that is not dependent upon the vertical, and this occurs in primeval art.

Their pictorial composition is not rational to our way of thinking. But they were nevertheless able to master the syntax of pictorial art.[1] It is simply that they had a different approach to art from the one to which we have become accustomed, ever since we accepted the dominance of the vertical and the horizontal, which—including their natural corollary, symmetry—have become so embedded in our consciousness that they seem to be an absolute condition of order.

This way of looking at things was unknown to prehistoric man, as indeed it still is to primitive peoples. Ambiguity, the existence of apparent contradictions and of the interweaving of events without regard to our sense of time (before and after) are the matters that find expression in primeval art.

What is it that differentiates the space conception of prehistory from that of the other periods? Are there any criteria that persisted throughout the whole period of prehistoric art?

It was almost by chance that I discovered how the prehistoric artist organized his composition and of his attitude towards space.

Not far from Les Eyzies lies the little museum of Laugerie Basse, situated directly under an overhanging curtain of rock. Laugerie Basse was one of the first sites excavated. The first discoverers of primeval art —a Frenchman and an Englishman, E. Lartet and H. Christy conducted

---

[1] Hoernes-Menghin, *op. cit.* page 127.

their excavations here in 1863, and reported their findings in their *Reliquiae Aquitanicae.*

In the little museum there was a triangular block of stone with incurving sides that caught my eye because of its shape. I took it out into the sunshine. It then became apparent that on the upper part of the left face and tilting downwards there was an engraved outline of a bull. (fig. 1) Its hindquarters disappeared into the stone together with the extremities of its hind legs. The line of its back was however very firmly engraved with a sharp kink at the position of the shoulder blades. As is so often the case in prehistoric works of art, the head was strongly moulded. At first glance it appeared as though the animal were grazing on a slightly convex ledge, with his strongly emphasized fore-legs resting on a lower level.

When I lifted up the stone to take it back, I turned it by chance round an angle of 180°. This enabled me to see that the curve of the ledge composed the neck and the chest of another animal which, in our way of looking at pictures, would be described as standing on its head. The stretched out neck and head of this gazelle-like creature stood out clearly in the altered angle of light. The rest of its body was only roughly indicated. Apparently the animal was depicted in flight. An outstretched fore leg lay alongside the head of the bull which, again due to the change of light, had disappeared—at least from our eyes. But the eyes of prehistoric man were free. He did not find it necessary to translate every composition into vertical parallels.

This carved block is certainly one of the less important works of the Magdalenian period, but through my chance turning of it I had seen the light make animals appear and disappear. This made me suddenly aware of the intentions of primeval art—of its principle of composition. It became clear to me that Paleolithic man looked at things and at space in a way different from that to which we have become accustomed.

Eskimos and Magdalenian Art
Some years later, when on a visit to Canada, I received additional confirmation of this from an anthropologist in the University of Toronto, E. S. Carpenter. Carpenter had lived for some time with the Aivilik Eskimos on the 20,000 square miles of Southampton Island north of Hudson Bay. In his essay 'Eskimo Space Concepts' he examines the space concepts of the Aivilik Eskimos in relation to their sense of direction, their views of the universe and above all their art.

The way of life of the Eskimo is roughly speaking similar to that of Magdalenian man in the Ice Age. The Eskimos are more 'primitive' than the North American Indians who show in their art that they have already

40

become dominated by vertical and horizontal and the need to organize these lines of direction upon a plane surface.

If an Aivilik Eskimo is given a photograph the wrong way up, he doesn't find it necessary to twist it around. When Eskimo children cannot complete their drawing upon a sheet of paper, they draw the rest of it upon the other side. This is similar to the way the Eskimos compose their engravings on bone or walrus teeth. They have a 'habit of scratching until a figure reaches the limits of the ivory, then turning the tusk over and completing the figure on the reverse side.'

'In handling these cribbage boards', says Carpenter 'I found myself turning them first this way, then that, orienting each figure in relation to myself. The Aivilik do not do this. Carvers draw a number of figures each oriented—by our standards—in a different direction.'

It is this manner of seeing things without any 'relation to myself' that distinguishes primeval art from all later art. It is not disorder but a different form of order that is being followed—an order to which we, in our sophistication, have lost the key.

Caverns Are Not Architecture
The dwellings of prehistoric man were not located in the interior of caves. They sheltered under overhanging rocks, as in Laugerie Haute and Laugerie Basse (Dordogne, France) and in the mouth of caves, as at Altamira (Spain), or just nearby, as in Comparelles (Dordogne, France) where, along a low corridor, dark stains have been found near fissures in the rock through which smoke could escape.

No traces of human dwellings have been found in the interior of the caverns. These were holy places in which, with the aid of magically potent pictures, the sacred rituals could be performed.

These caverns owed their existence to the forces of erosion which often endowed them with fantastic formations. Sometimes surfaces had been polished smooth by sand and water. The heavy clay sank to the ground but also, in many cases, adhered to walls and ceilings. After the period of upheaval, drops of hard calcareous water from mountain streams filtered through the ceilings and gradually deposited translucent curtains over the walls or formed columns which grew from the top down or from the ground up until after they met in the middle.

In some of the caverns where tourists are not permitted to enter and which have remained undisturbed throughout tens of thousands of years, dreamlike crystal growths arise from the ground—thickly clustered, white as snow and fine as needles—as in the Tuc d'Audoubert (Pyrenees, France). These fantastic subterranean caverns undoubtedly breathe an

41

air of marvel and mystery. But one must beware. These caverns, which are the containers of primeval art, have nothing to do with architecture.

Everyone is free to interpret the fantastic forms occurring in these caverns as cathedrals, banquet halls, galleries, chapels or what have you, but actually these uninterrupted sequences of forms, sometimes sharply defined, utterly amorphous, have no connection whatever with architecture.

Vaults, so high that they are beyond the reach of the beam of light from one's lantern, alternate with tube-like passages, so low that one must crawl painfully along them; with sudden abysses; with great boulders and with falls of rubble. Further, the caverns only possess an interior, they have no exterior. In all this they are quite different from the architecture later invented by man.

These caverns possess no space in our meaning of this word, for in them perpetual darkness reigns. The caverns are, spatially speaking, empty. This is well appreciated by anyone who has tried alone to find his way out from one of them. The weak beam of light from his torch is swallowed up by the absolute darkness around him, while rocky tunnels and crumbling slopes repeat themselves in every direction and re-echo his question: where is the outlet from this labyrinth?

Light and the Art of the Caverns
Nothing is more destructive of the true values of primeval art than the glare of electric light in this realm of eternal night.[1] Flares or small stone lamps burning animal fat, of which examples have been found, only permit one to obtain fragmentary glimpses of the colours and lines of the objects depicted. In such a soft flickering light these take on an almost magical movement. The engraved lines, and even the coloured surfaces, lose their intensity under a strong light, and sometimes disappear altogether. Only a soft side-lighting—lumière frisée—can awaken their original strength. Only in this way can the fine veining of the drawings be seen unsmothered by their rough background.

Maybe enough has now been said to show that prehistoric man did not associate the caverns with architecture. In his view the caverns simply provided him with places that he could use for his magic arts. He selected these places with the utmost care. Some were perhaps chosen because the rock formation seemed particularly suitable. But most were chosen because he believed them to possess special powers. There were no fixed rules.

However, one predisposition can be detected that recurs repeatedly. This is that prehistoric man did not consider the caverns as an edifice

---

[1] It is unfortunately often necessary to use flash bulbs when taking photographs in the caverns, but whenever at all possible we always used softer lights with reflectors.

to be decorated: secret signs and figurations are placed in positions that are extremely difficult of access, and at the uttermost end of the caves, where the walls narrow to a mere crack. In these cases it is clear that prehistoric man was more anxious to hide his artistic creations than to expose them. They came and went in the dim light of his flickering lamps. The tradition of secreting the most sacred manifestations in places accessible only to the initiated persisted in the Egyptian temples, where the statue of the god was concealed in a dark cell at the furthest extremity of the temple. No-one but the king and the high priest had access to this place. What in prehistory was provided by nature has here become translated into architecture.

Once it has become clear that prehistoric man did not look upon the caverns as an architectural space we can realise the freedom with which he was able to employ natural materials for his purposes, and the new concept of prehistoric space conception begins to emerge: the unfettered imaginative power with which prehistoric man handles surfaces and his attitude towards them.

Freedom of Approach to All Surfaces
The surfaces of the caverns and overhanging cliffs are sometimes flat and sometimes curved. They change continually in their form and in their direction, sometimes also in their colour. This is particularly true of the limestone rocks and caverns of the Dordogne—that centre of primeval art. Here the rock walls are as smoothly polished as though a glacier had passed over them. The surfaces are however never regular. The rock walls curve gently in every possible direction.

This multiformity of the surfaces, their infinite freedom of direction and perpetual change, is at the basis of all primeval art, which is closer than any other to Nature but still knows how to preserve the essential individuality of human existence.

It would, despite everything, have been possible to select vertical and horizontal planes. But this was never done. None of the variously sloping surfaces receives any preference. To be chosen, a surface must possess some magical properties. In any case primeval art is not used to 'decorate' a space in our way of thinking. In prehistory man was completely unfettered in the way in which he selected surfaces.

This is why we have to free ourselves as much as possible from the way of looking at things that has been part of our inheritance for thousands of years, if we wish to come near to an understanding of primeval art. The lines and orientation of a picture has no relation to the horizontal or vertical; nor is the selection of the surface dependent upon its angle

FIG. 1

44

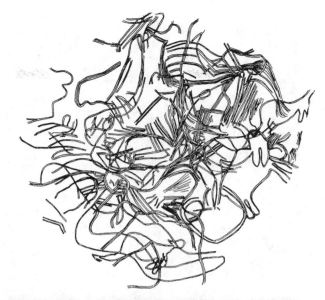

FIG. 3B

FIG. 3A

46

FIG. 4

47

of inclination. Whether the structure and shape of the surface be smooth, curved or cracked one can always see an ability to use it to the full.

The Pech-Merle Ceiling

Only a few instances can be noted here. On the damp clay ceiling of the so-called Salle des Hiéroglyphes (fig. 2) in the cavern of Pech-Merle which measures about 10 by 4 meters, generation after generation in Aurignacian times drew with their fingers the outlines of supplicatory figures, superimposing them one upon the other: mammoths, bird-headed goddesses and some fragments of other beings. These were carefully copied and deciphered by their discoverer Abbé Lemozi. He worked lying upon his back in a most hazardous situation, upon the smooth and slippery rocks which lay under the ceiling and sloped away into nothingness. The designs upon this ceiling, which date from the beginnings of art, are suspended above a void. Here there can have been no question of decorating a space.

Many millenia later, the same phenomenon appears upon the ceiling of the cavern of Altamira, which represents the apex of Magdalenian art. This rock vault is only five feet from the ground, so it is impossible to stand upright beneath it. A pathway has therefore been dug out for visitors to walk along. Over this low vault spread the famous frescos with their animals and gigantic symbols, which on one side merge into the earth. To get a good view of this ceiling one must lie stretched out upon the original level of the floor. Even then it is not possible for the eye to take in the structure of the entire composition at one glance. It was not created for the public nor to decorate a space: it is magic which exists for itself.

Neither the slightly curved Pech-Merle ceiling, from the earliest period, nor the Altamira ceiling, from the period of highest artistic knowledge in prehistory, span any architectural space. Each exists for itself alone, hovering independently over the hollow space below. (fig. 3)

The Lascaux Gallery

Curved and winding surfaces are handled in a similar way. Sometimes naturally formed arches and passages take on such regular shapes that they appear to be the work of human hands. The dome-like vault and branching passages of Lascaux are like this. The ceilings are composed of very thick non-porous limestone. Through condensation they became entirely covered with tiny lime crystals which provide a magnificently solid painting surface. The walls, on the other hand, are impossible to paint on, being made up of brittle rock with horizontal cracks.

The dome, with its frieze of gigantic animals, as well as the passage that leads almost axially from it (called, from its position, the *diverticule*

48

axial) both show the manner of handling curved surfaces. (fig. 4) The tunnel-like passage is particularly instructive. At first sight the semi-circular vault of the near part of its roof, with its luminous colours and crystalline background, has almost the appearance of a gallery in an Italian Baroque castle. Closer observation shows however that the same attitude has been adopted in painting this curving, concave surface that stretches away into the distance, as was used in making the minute Magdalenian engravings upon rounded pieces of bone. The red-brown primeval cattle, yellow and black horses, punctuations and other magical signs, are all freely disposed at varying angles, and yet one cannot help realizing that there is a general sense of composition. This can be instanced by the dynamic organization of the tapering heads and necks of three red-brown cattle. The rest of their bodies curve over the ceiling. The group is joined by a yellow 'chinese' pony, drawn to quite another scale, and a stream of other animals stretches away to right and left.

This different way of looking at things is just what interests us today: the way in which prehistoric man could grasp things in their entirety without needing to organise them according to a static viewpoint or to adjust them to the vertical. This is brought out by the position given to a red bull in this sloping passage. To our eyes he appears to be leaping over a chasm.

Probably Magdalenian man saw no leap and no abyss. He simply saw a third animal who came to join the other two. This follows the same principle of vision as was shown on the carved triangular block of Laugerie Basse.

At the very end of the *diverticule axial* at Lascaux are a number of horses. One of them 'has fallen over backwards with all four feet in the air'. This horse, who has 'tumbled over a precipice', has been interpreted as evidence of an animal tragedy, well known in Solutrean times, when herds of wild horses were driven over cliffs. But here, too, it would seem that one should be cautious about such naturalistic interpretations. It is probable that the horse at Lascaux has no more fallen into an abyss than the multi-coloured bison at Castillo is climbing vertically up a stalacmite.

This bison can be found in the second chamber of the cavern at Castillo which lies a few hundred yards from La Pasiega. The bold carving of his powerful loins strikes one immediately on entering the hall because of the deep dent thus made in one of the stalacmite columns, which distinguishes it from all the others that surround it. A nearer view shows that some parts of the animal: tail, flanks, the outline of the back and the belly, 'sont formés par un accident rocheaux' as was noted by

Alcalde del Rio, who discovered this cavern in 1903, and Abbé Breuil who first described and illustrated it.[1]

Irregular Convex Surfaces: Castillo and Altamira

As is universally the case in primeval art, the eye of the Ice Age hunter discovers images of the animals he seeks in the structure of the rocks. The French describe this recognition of natural formations as 'épouser les contours'. A few lines, a little carving or some colour are enough to bring the animal into view.

In Altamira a Magdalenian artist was able to transform the hideous excrescences from the ceiling into bison—lying, falling or standing—with a mastery of line and colour hitherto unknown. (fig. 3)

Several hundred years earlier, the slight carving of the vertical buffalo of Castillo gives evidence of the same principle: the power to handle irregular surfaces with complete freedom. Whether the animal appears in a vertical position or in any other position is quite irrelevant to the eye of prehistoric man.

In forming the Castillo bison, the artist proceeded from the natural shapes before him. He carved in the hind hoofs very precisely, just beneath the swelling flanks; he strengthened the natural outline of the hindquarters and the belly, and he added with a bit of black colour the mane and the lower parts. The animal's small head, lightly sketched in horns and painted nose almost disappear into the rock. All emphasis was concentrated on the tension of his sinewy body.

Sloping Surfaces: the Bisons of Tuc d'Audoubert

Freedom of approach to all surfaces, regardless of horizontal or vertical direction is a basic principle of primeval art. This is shown again in the unusual situation, when the background for a work of art had first had to be prepared, in the case of the two bison modelled in high relief in the *sancta sanctorum* of the cavern of Tuc d'Audoubert. These bison were modelled upon an inclined plane. Their base is a block of rock fallen from the ceiling. In their almost inaccessible, but most carefully considered situation at the farthest end of the cavern, these two animals have been moulded upon the rock in the damp clay of the cavern. They could just as easily have been modelled in a vertical position, but they were not. The inclined plane heightens the impressiveness of this fertility rite, and makes the mounting position of the male animal terrifyingly vivid, as well as the freedom of approach of primeval art to the surface plane.

Since the discovery of this cavern of Tuc d'Audoubert in 1912 by Count

1 H. Alcalde del Rio, Abbé Henri Breuil, R. Père Lorezo Sierra, *Les Cavernes de la Région Cantabrique (Espagne)*. Monaco 1912, page 149, plates 75 and 76.

Henri Begouen and his two sons, nothing equal to it has been found. Henri Begouen, at that time professor of paleontology in the University of Toulouse, has described this route so vividly that it is better to let him tell, in his own words, how in this cavern one does not clamber downhill but must scramble steeply up narrow chimneys and across great halls before reaching the bison pair.

C'est tout à fait au fond d'un des couloirs élevés de la caverne du Tuc d'Audoubert, à 700 mètres au moins de l'entrée, que nous avons trouvé, mes fils et moi, le 10 Octobre 1912, des statues d'argile représentant des bisons.

L'accès de cette galerie terminale est des plus difficile. L'entrée même de la caverne est défendue par un bief formé par la résurgence du Volp. Il faut pénétrer en barque sous terre. . . avant de trouver des galeries parsemées de flaques d'eau, mais où l'on peut à la rigueur au temps des basses eaux passer à pied sec. [The cavern] se compose en somme de trois étages: il y a d'abord celui qui est au niveau de l'eau; on accède au second, à environ 150 mètres de l'entrée en escaladant une petite falaise de 2 mètres de haut; là s'ouvre une galerie qui s'élargit en vastes salles ornées de superbes concrétions calcaires d'une éblouissante blancheur et affectant les formes les plus pittoresques. . . . Enfin, dans un coin d'une des salles, se trouve une cheminée d'abord droite puis s'incurvant en hélice vers le haut. Il fallut escalader cet à-pic de 12 m. 50, en s'agrippant aux aspérités de la roche. . . . Le couloir qui s'ouvre à cet étage est étroit et accidenté. En certains endroits des animaux peu nombreux sont gravés sur les parois. . . . Le fond de cette salle très étroit et très basse de plafond était obstrué par des piliers de stalectite qui empêchaient tout passage, mais permettaient de voir que la galerie continuait au-delà. Mes fils . . . brisèrent trois de ces colonnes. Ils pratiquèrent ainsi une ouverture . . . par laquelle on put passer en rampant.

After this they went through several halls until they came to the final obstacle: 'une sorte de falaise d'argile où l'on voit des traces du passage des hommes et des ours. Pour se retentir sur ces pentes glissantes les ours ont incrusté profondément leurs griffes qui ont marqué des sillons longs et tortueux. Leurs poils même ont laissé leur empreinte.'

Finally they saw in the clay 'des empreintes de talons humains. . . . Il s'est déposé sur l'argile une legère pellicule de stalagmite d'un grain très fin, de l'épaisseur d'une coquille d'œuf, et qui a admirablement moulé ces empreintes. . . . J'en arrive à me demander si nous ne sommes pas là en présence de traces de quelque cérémonie magique. . . . Nous sommes d'ailleurs tout près du fond de la caverne, qui pouvait être une sorte de sanctuaire.'

51

It was the sanctuary of the pair of bison. The question whether there was any feeling of composition and artistic sense of emphasis in the primeval period is here answered with a rare clarity.

First there is a stream which flows into the cavern and then suddenly disappears under the ground. In the cavern of Tuc d'Audoubert itself one must climb through three levels before one reaches an entrance that bears the impress of feet of the Magdalenian period. These heel marks lead one to believe that this is a place similar to the *Salle des Hiéroglyphes* at Pech-Merle, with the bird-goddesses upon the ceiling. Finally, at the uttermost end of the cavern, beneath a high vaulted roof, the pair of bison have been placed upon a kind of altar. Their modelling is so strong that it emanates an extraordinary sense of space although in fact their size is surprisingly small: the bull being 63 cms long and the cow 61 cms (24½ inches and 23¾ inches).

Summary
The distinguishing mark of the space conception of primeval art is the complete independence and freedom of its vision which has never again been attained in later periods. In our sense there is no above and no below, no clear distinction of separateness from an intermingling and also certainly no rules of proportional size. Gigantic animals of the Magdalenian era stand alongside tiny deer from Aurignacian times, as for example on the dome of Lascaux. Violent juxtaposition in size as well as in time are accepted as a matter of course. All is within the continuous present, the perpetual interflow of today, yesterday and tomorrow.

Every prehistoric work of art is a proof of this. Whenever possible previous designs are not destroyed but the lines of both earlier and later works intermingle till they sometimes—but only to our eyes—appear inextricable. It was recognized quite early that this superimposition was not due to idle chance but to a deliberate reluctance to destroy the past. Peyrony and Capitan who, in the early days of this century, explored the most important cavern of the Dordogne, even then pointed out that 'Wherever one finds drawings of different periods superimposed upon one another, the last ones, though they bear no relation to the others, never destroy them more than is absolutely necessary for their own execution. The older drawings were never deliberately destroyed. On the contrary they were respected almost as though they were sacred.'[1]

Primeval art was made by nomads. This being so it is a matter for wonder that many of the caverns contain works ranging from the beginning to the end of prehistory—from the Aurignacian to the Azilian eras. This is a period far outside the range of our limited conception of time.

1 Capitan et Peyrony: *L'Humanité primitive dans la région des Eysies*, Paris 1924, pages 95/96.

What Were the Next Developments?

History discloses that a space conception—man's attitude towards space —is maintained over long periods of time which, in other respects, may show great changes. It is unfortunately not possible here to develop this theme or to give more than a very few indications of subsequent developments.

Before the dawn of the historical period, a tremendous revolution had taken place in man's manner of perception. A relationship to an unlimited number of directions is replaced by a single relationship: to the VERTICAL. The Horizontal is merely its essential counterpart. With the ever greater dominance of the vertical, parallel sequences, the axis, symmetry, all came into being; all of which were unknown to primeval art.

The enthusiasm with which ancient Egyptian art adopted the vertical and the repetition of the vertical as a means of artistic expression can be seen in the bas reliefs of the tomb of Ti at Sakkarah, one of the finest works of the Old Kingdom. When Ti, a high dignitary of the 5th Dynasty, goes out in his boat to hunt in the papyrus swamp, the papyrus stems behind him are ranged so regularly and so tightly together that he appears as though before a background of corrugated cardboard. In the 6th Dynasty tomb of Mererouka also at Sakkarah, the phalanx of vertical lines appears even more strongly accentuated.

All lineal directions are dominated by the vertical, and also all *surfaces* are subordinated to the vertical plane. Everything is arranged in relation to this. Again the horizontal plane is but the necessary complement. Every object is adjusted to fit into either a vertical or a horizontal direction. From the beginning of Egyptian art to the time of the New Kingdom one often finds objects depicted in both horizontal and vertical projections in the same picture.

A slate palette in the Cairo Museum of around 3000 B. C. depicts the conquest of seven walled cities. The walls are all shown from above, the interior of the cities partly from above and partly laid out flat.

When a primitive shrine of this period is depicted, all parts of the sanctuary are ranged next to one another along a vertical plane. It is hard for our eyes to gain from this a spatial conception of the building. It is first necessary for us to translate it into three-dimensional perspective.[1]

Later on, in the time of the New Kingdom, great subtlety was exercised in the simultaneous projection of objects in both vertical and horizontal planes.

---

[1] A. Badaway, *Egyptian Architecture*. Cairo, 1954, plate 22.

In a painting of a garden of about 1400 B.C. (in the British Museum) with palms, fruit trees and a rectangular pool, the fish and water birds within it are shown on a vertical plane, the pool remains horizontal, as seen in plan, and the trees which surround it like the sides of a box, are laid out flat.

To the eye of the contemporary Egyptian these pictures were certainly not as difficult to see as they are for us. They did not appear to him to be flat, for he at once translated them into three dimensional form.

Instead of the freedom of line and the freedom of surface that we find in prehistory, we have a union of line with surface and the subordination of all representation to the vertical or horizontal planes. The absolute dominance of the vertical was a ruling principle during the time of the first great empire states, and almost became a symbol of a strongly hierarchical social order.

Primeval Art and Modern Art

The reason that we can now slowly understand the space conception of primeval art is due to the work of contemporary artists. Painters like Kandinsky and Klee have opened our eyes to the realization that the organization of a picture is not exclusively dependent upon the strength of the vertical, but that there can also be a free play of the elements of the picture quite independent from it.

In the early works of Kandinsky, which are full of the passion of this new revelation, lines and colour are no longer under the domination of the vertical (one of the most significant examples is his 'Weisse Ecke', 1913 in the Museum of Non Objective Painting, New York). One senses a striving for a cosmic expression, for just that freedom of line and freedom of surface that is so strikingly present in primeval art.

Whether one looks at the Salle des Hiéroglyphes of Pech-Merle, with its interwining figurations, or the Altamira ceiling, with its powerful sequence of animals intimately associated with undecipherable symbols, the space conception of primeval art always remains the same. It is not chaos; it approaches more nearly to the order of the stars that move about in endless space, universal in their relations and unconfined by any vertical.

Sigfried Giedion

We see blues ranging from blue-greens to blue-purples in a variety of tints, tones, and shades, but the word 'blue' without qualification is probably, at any given time, a constant for each individual. The colour-word seldom stands alone, the colour perception never (Red Cross, red herring). Colour-names occasionally stand alone, with meanings widely divergent from the colour word, *e.g.*, 'He's a yellow Red.'

Colours may be aggressive, warm, advancing, or cool, retiring, passive, the reasons for this categorization being, for man at least, sociological and learned. The broadness of this division of the spectrum militates against colour being used alone as a specific symbol. Just as the colour-word must be linked to another word for the symbol to be specific, so the perceived colour must appear in a certain shape, *e.g.*, the Purple Heart, or in a specific situation, *e.g.*, a white shirt, flown from a beleagured fort or from a clothes line on blue Monday.

The primitive, like the child, loves strong colour. Since, for him, each colour has symbolic meaning, they are rarely mixed. This, plus pigment scarcity, tend to make the observed colour and its visualization from the spoken colour-word very similar. Today's technology permits us to colour in thousands of ways but few of these colours are of any use as symbols. Response is always strong to chroma and a dilution may be psychologically reflected in meaning, *e.g.*, 'parlour pink' for a left-wing political dilettante.

No one has a specific colour memory. Twenty-two art students were asked to paint from memory a sample of Coca Cola red, a standard colour formulated by Du Pont; the results varied from orange reds to red violets. Other experiments suggested that the more the original colour departed from purity the less successful were the results. This lack of specific colour memory lays stress upon the object half of the colour symbol. It also suggests that the closer the colour is to a common denominator concept of, green for example, the more successful it is as a symbol.

Man never sees an individual colour. All surface colour varies as it presents a changing face to the light. It also changes as parts of the surface reflect coloured backgrounds. In addition, an eye nerve, sensitive to one colour, but only one of a bundle of approximately a million nerves, is involved in 'cross talk'. Thus nerves involved in the sensation of other colours are automatically activated so that no single colour is sensed at one time. Finally, seldom in life is a colour area large enough to occupy the whole of the retina—and red with green is very different from red with yellow.

The only time a single colour exists is when it is mental—conjured up by the appropriate colour-word. Colour as symbol exists almost totally in the area of the verbal.

Harley Parker

A particularly important place in the general theory of sign should be given, I think, to the distinction between logic-sign and magic-sign. By logic-sign I mean a sign operating under certain functional conditions through which it is a sign for the intellect, whether speculative or practical: that is, when the predominance of the intellect defines a particular psychological or cultural regime. Under such conditions, the sign, be it in itself sensible or intellectual, speaks ultimately to the intellect and refers ultimately to a psychic regime ruled by the intellect.

I call magic-sign a sign operating under a different functional regime where it speaks primarily to the imagination regarded as a supreme and ruling standard of the psychological or cultural life as a whole. The sign, be it in itself sensible or intellectual, ultimately speaks to the imaginative

faculties and refers ultimately to a psychic regime emerged in the vitilizing depth of the imagination.

My working hypothesis deals here with the notion of functional conditions or states. I am using the word 'state' here in a sense similar to that intended by chemists when they speak of the solid, liquid and gaseous states of matter, or by theologians when they speak of the state of pure nature, the state of innocence, and so forth. In an essay on *Sign and*

Symbol published in 1938 I suggested that a fundamental distinction must be made between the state of our developed cultures and another state in which, for the psychic and cultural life as a whole, the last word rests with the imagination as supreme and final law. No doubt the intellect is present, but in a way it is not free. That is a kind of state I am calling the magic regime of psychic and cultural life and which is linked with the magic-sign of which I just spoke.

May I add that this working hypothesis was lucky enough to reconcile opposed points of view in a particularly controversial field? Some time before his death Professor Lucien Lévy-Bruhl, who was one of my dearest professors when I was young, was so kind to write to me of his agreement on this point. 'As you put it rightly', he said, 'primitive mentality is a state of human mentality and I can accept the characteristics through which you define it.' And he went on to say that he had never intended to oppose the primitive mind and our civilized mind as to specifically and structurally different types of mind.

Animals make use of signs; they live in a kind of magical world. Biologically united to nature, they use signs which belong to a psychic regime which is entirely imaginative. The intellect in primitive man is of the same kind as ours. It may even be more alive in him than in some more civilized people. But the question here is that of its status and of the existential conditions under which it operates.

The whole mental regime of primitive man is under the authority of imagination. In him the intellect is in every way involved with, and dependent on, the imagination and its savage world. This kind of mental regime is one where acquaintance with nature is experienced and lived through with an intensity and to an extent we cannot easily picture. This is a state of inferiority, but it is by no means despicable— it is a human state—the state of mankind in its infancy, a fertile state through which we have had to pass. Under this regime, humanity enriched itself with many vital truths, a number of which were perhaps lost when it passed on to an adult stage. These truths were known by way of dream or instinct and by actual participation in the thing known, just as if we imagined that in the knowledge that a bee has of the world of flowers, a light which the bee does not possess, the light of reason and of the intellect, were present in a diffused, undifferentiated state before becoming condensed into stars and solar systems separating the light from darkness. Here we meet with a difficulty analogous to that which we find when we try to penetrate the mental life of animals. Whatever we picture to ourselves is bathed in intelligence and in intelligence which is free in civilized intelligence. We have great trouble in depicting to ourselves what another kind of mental life can be like, and if we are disciples of Descartes it is strictly impossible for us to do so.

Let me say in brief that in our logical state, sensations, images and ideas are solar, bound up with the luminous regular life of the intellect and its laws of gravitation. In the magic state they were nocturnal, bound up with fluid and twilight mental life of the imagination and of an experience which was astonishingly powerful but entirely lived through and dreamed. The same is true of the sign and of the relation of sign to the thing signified. Since truth is a relation of the cognitive faculty to the thing and belongs only to the judgement of the intellect which grasps it as such, it should be said that in primitive man this relation is experienced but is not winnowed out for its own sake. It is known, of course, because the intellect is present, but it is known in a nocturnal manner since intelligence is, in this case, immersed in the powers of imagination.

When we consider the primitive man we may say that in him the relation of the mind to the thing is ambivalent. The same relation is false in the eyes of our evolved consciousness to the extent that it asserts for instance the existence of composite tribal ancestors, like duckmen or kangaroo men, and this relation is true to the same extent that it affirms the vital union of man and nature of which this myth is the symbol, but for primitive man a distinction of this kind has no meaning. This is because his very adhesion to truth is not ours, since for him the idea of truth has not been winnowed out for itself. He adheres *en bloc*, at the same time, and indistinctly to the symbol and the symbolized. Here is for him, in indivisible fashion, an image or a likeness of truth, an equivalent, an *als ob* of truth, without his having winnowed out the idea of truth for its own sake. In similar fashion, a child believes in a story, in the *Adventures of Alice in Wonderland*. Awaken the child, withdraw him from the world of the imagination and he knows very well that a little girl cannot enter a rabbit hole; but primitive man does not awaken. He is not yet withdrawn from the motherly bosom of the imagination which makes him familiar with the whole of nature and without which he could not face the relentless severity of his existence as a cave-dweller at war with beasts. He lives in the world of make-believe.

Henri Bergson has admirably shown that what is to be found as a source and basis of magic, as a primordial element, is the relationship of causality: 'Man', he says, 'realized at once that the limits of his normal influence over the outside world were soon reached and he could not resign himself to going no further, so he carried on the movement and since the movement could not by itself secure the desired result, nature must needs take the task in hand. Things will then be more or less charged with submissiveness and potency. They will hold at our disposal a power which yields to the desires of man and of which man may avail himself. The working of magic begins the act which man cannot finish. They go through the motions which alone could not produce the desired effect but which will achieve it if the man concerned knows how to prevail upon the goodwill of things. Magic is then innate in man, being but the outward projection of a desire which fills the heart.'

That which I believe to be lacking in Bergson's theory is that it does not take into account the indispensible instrument of magical activity, the practical sign. It is surely true that magic implies an appeal to some cosmic power which brings a desire of man to a happy outcome, an appeal which itself presupposes some sympathy, some compliance in things, but it must be added that magic makes use of signs. Here the relationship proper to the sign and to the practical sign necessarily intervenes. Man does not merely outline some casual action: he makes a sign to semi-personal cosmic elements. It is needful that we insist upon the mental characteristics of these practical signs, subject as they are to the nocturnal regime of the imagination.

First of all, in my opinion, we here find ourselves confronted with a refraction in the world of imagination or with a nocturnal deformation of the practical sign as a quality of sign, or considered in order of the relationship itself to signification. That is to say, in the order of formal causality, wherein the sign is by its essence the vicar of the object. Let us not forget that this relationship of sign to signified is in its own order singularly clothed. The motion towards the sign or the image, St. Thomas says, after Aristotle, is identical with the motion toward the object itself: 'Sic enim est unus et idem motus in imaginem cum illo qui est in re.'

In the formal objective order the sign is thus something most astonishing whereas the routine of culture alone prevents our wonder. In this marvelous function of containing the object with respect to the mind or of having present in itself the thing itself in another kind of existence is fully exercised in primitive man. Words are not anaemic or colourless; they are overflowing with life, with their life as signs for the primitive man. But that in itself sets a snare for his imagination. Thanks to the condition of experience and lived participation wherein he has established his own mental life, the presence as to knowledge of the signified in the sign becomes for him a presence as to reality, a physical intersociability, a physical fusion and a physical equivalent of the sign and the signified: invocation of mythical names, magic objects, spells idolatry, and so forth. Primitive man is intoxicated with the excellence of the sign. Yet the sign never altogether loses its genuine relationship of signification to some other thing. The idol is god, and yet never altogether god. Then again a slurring takes place from formal objective causality to efficient causality. The creation of signs is a mark of the preeminence of the mind, and the instinct and the intelligence quickly informed man that symbols make him enter into the path of things in order to know them. At once, in a psychic regime wherein the imagination is dominant, this slurring will take place. Man will think that symbols make us enter into the heart of things in order to act physically upon them and in order to make them physically subject to us and in order to effect for us a real and physical union with them.

Moreover, are not the signs in question first and foremost practical signs? At once the imagination will mistake a sign directive toward an operation for an operating sign, and why should we be astonished that the imagination of primitive man cannot distinguish between formal causality and efficient causality, when the intelligence of philosophers so often confuses them.

The sign, then, not only makes men know things, it makes things be. It is an efficient cause in itself; hence all the procedures of sympathetic magic. In order to make rain fall to the ground, the sorcerer waters the ground; in order to obtain abundant tubers, he buries in the ground, at seed time, magical stones of the same shape as the desired tubers—these will teach the yams and the tubers to grow big, to reach the same size as the stones. The stones make them a sign; they are patterns, symbols. The theory of mana or orenda, the theory of force spread throughout nature wherein all things participate in various degrees, seems to be the fruit of a later reflection upon this use of the sign to the extent that reflection will be intensified; the idea of the semi-physical, semi-moral environment will become more and more materialized, but finally, a sign, in spite of everything, remains a sign. Inevitably there will take place a return of the order of causality to which it belongs: that is of formal causality and of the relationship of signification which, with primitive man, becomes a relationship of fusion and of physical equivalence upon the relationship of efficient causality and of operation, and the imagination will oscillate from one way of thinking the sign to the other. In the perspective of efficient causality there is a distinction, a difference between the cause and the effect as well as between the sign and the signified. In the perspective of formal causality the nature by the imagination and of that intoxication which the sign induced in primitive man by the relationship of signification, there is a physical inter-penetration and fusion of the sign and the signified. Since we are by hypothesis dealing with a nocturnal regime of the imagination and since for the imagination as such, as dreams bear witness, the principle of identity does not exist, and then again since the intelligence is still present, bound up with and clothed in the imagination, it is easy to understand that for primitive man the identity of things is constantly unmade and made again. It is altogether too hasty for us to say that with him there is simply an identity between the sign and the signified. No, there is an oscillation, there is a going and coming from distinction to identification. When children play by building sand castles, these castles are truly *castles* for them. If you trample them, the children will cry with rage and indignation, but once their play is at an end, what were castles are only sand. Primitive man believes to be identical, through the living power of the imagination, that which he obscurely knows to be different through his intelligence bound up in the imagination. It is impossible, I think, to understand anything about his thought if it be conceived from the point of view of the logical or daylight state of the intelligence taken as the ruling measure of all thought. It is the thought of an awakened dreamer wherein the role of play and the allowance of play is tremendously great.

If the previous remarks are true, we may conclude that language began in mankind in the form of magical language. To the mind of the primitive man the word does not signify a concept and through the concept a thing. It directly signifies a thing, and the word and the thing it signifies are both distinct and one, for the word, insofar as it remains a sign (formal causality) is not physically the thing, and insofar as it is a magical sign—confusion between formal and efficient causality—the word is physically the thing or causes the thing to exist. Nothing is more natural for primitive mentality than to make the name into a real equivalent of the thing named, and to have a patient as confident in swallowing the prescription as in swallowing the medicine itself, and the cover of the deceit and illusion of magical thought, at least the dignity and sacred mystery of the words, were felt and recognized even though exceedingly overrated. Once the mind and the society have passed under the solar regime of intelligence, the sense of this dignity and sacred mystery, now purified of its magical connotation, remains essential to human civilization. Yet the sense in question diminishes and is endangered in proportion as civilization, especially industrial civilization, becomes more artificial and loses direct contact with the world of nature and when civilization decays, the sense of the dignity and mystery of words dissipates and is finally lost. Then, in order to recover it, poetry may possibly be tempted to return to magic and to crave for 'the power of words', as Allen Tate puts in his telling essay on *Poe and the Power of Words*, and as can be seen in Mallarmé and many other modern poets, especially German and French romanticists and contemporary surrealists.

At this point in our analysis we must be particularly careful. Though poetic knowledge bears in itself no trace of magic in the strict sense, nevertheless it knows things as one with the self and as resounding in the subjectivity and in its expression it is, to a certain extent, subjected to the nocturnal regime of the imagination, so that the thought of the poet, at least his unconscious thought, resembles somewhat the mental activity of the primitive man in the ways of magic in the large sense of this word. The Belgium poet Verheeren was a friend of Lévy-Bruhl. After receiving his book he wrote to him that he was all the more interested in this description of primitive mentality as he recognized in it a genuine description of his own way of thinking. While it is not at all of this general resemblance with the regime of the magical thought that I am now speaking, it is of an effort of the poet to bring about a magical operation through poetry and to transmute or conquer reality or to reach a state of fusion with reality by the creative power of words by using words as magical signs.

A curious and tragic phenomenon where something great and invaluable is looked for and missed, namely the genuine dignity of words, which refers to truth, not to power, and where by dint of refinement the civilized mind retrogresses to that magical notion of the sign which was normally in the child-like state of mankind yet is for mankind in its adult state, but a pathological symptom.

Jacques Maritain

SOVIET TELEVISION

Television is being widely extended in the Soviet Union all the time.
Today the country has fifteen television stations and by the end of the
year many more will be in operation. The basic principle we are guided
by in making up programs is to help to satisfy the constantly rising
cultural requirements of the Soviet people. The finest theatres, circuses,
museums, stadiums, and the best art, scientific, and sports collectives
are always glad to take part in telecasts.

In the USSR television serves the aims of cultural development, technical
progress, the struggle for peace, and the consolidation of the friendship
of the peoples. Telecasts tell of life in the USSR and abroad, disseminate
political and scientific knowledge, deal extensively with the peaceful
pursuits of Soviet people and with accomplishments in art and literature.
Appearing before TV audiences are prominent scientists and front-rank
people in industry, well-known public figures, and commentators on
international events. Plays and concerts are telecast from the studio, as
well as from theatres and concert halls, and sports contests are telecast
from stadiums. Thanks to television, the best stage plays become available
to the widest sections of the population. The Central Studio's work
may serve as an illustration of our programs:

Last year the Moscow Television Centre presented 187 dramatic and musical plays, more than 100 concerts, 219 feature films, 450 newsreels and other documentary films, 66 sports, 160 political and other public and scientific telecasts. It acquainted audiences not only with plays on the boards of the capital's theatres, but also with plays given by theatres from other towns and countries on tours in the Soviet Union. Among those shown were Chekhov's *Three Sisters*, Gorky's *The Lower Depths*, *The Philistines*, and *The Barbarians*, and Tolstoi's *Anna Karenina*, *Resurrection*, and *The Living Corpse* of Russian classical plays; the Soviet dramaturgists plays: *The Break-up* by Lavrenyev, *Northern Dawn* by Nikitin, and *The Unforgettable Year 1919* by Vishnevsky; and plays by foreign playwrights: Hugo's *Ruy Blas* and *Les Miserables*, Shakespeare's *Two Gentlemen of Verona* and *Much Ado about Nothing*, Balzac's *Eugenie Grandet*, *The Grey-haired Girl* by Li Tsing Chi and Ting Ni, and *The Devil's Mill* by Jan Drda.

Also frequently telecast are operas and ballets, operettas and theme concerts, acquainting audiences with the latest musical works, music of the peoples of the USSR and the best performers. The screen also regularly acquaints audiences with amateur art, which has had exceptionally wide development in the Soviet Union.

Telecasts on political and other public questions occupy an important place. Presented in easily comprehensible language, these acquaint audiences with the more important events in the Soviet Union as well as abroad, the achievements of the front-rank people in industry and agriculture, the attainments of Soviet science and engineering, and the latest sports news in the USSR and other countries.

Literary and art festivals of the Union Republics held in Moscow, performances by theatres and soloists from other towns, important dates widely observed in the country, and premieres of Moscow theatres—are all reflected in the telecasting plan.

Even from this cursory review of the content of Soviet television programs one can see what a big part it plays in meeting the cultural requirements of the people. The Moscow Studio receives hundreds of letters daily which comment on shows and make requests. These are carefully studied and the wishes expressed taken into consideration. At the suggestion of audiences the Central Studio started a monthly journal, *Art*, which gives news of literature, the theatre, painting, and so on. Appearing in this journal are prose writers, poets, essayists, playwrights, composers, film directors, actors and scenery painters who tell of the latest works of Soviet and foreign writers, of what theatres are doing about new repertories, and of their preparations to present Russian and foreign classical plays and music.

Special programs for children are given on Sundays and weekdays in the evening before adult programs are presented. Soviet producers are constantly seeking new forms of telecasts for children and young people. The plays help to implant in children love for and devotion to country and lofty moral qualities by showing examples of courageous and noble deeds and revealing the heroic quality of everyday work. Telecasts for children pursue the aim of helping parents and the school to educate children and broaden their outlook, to develop in them good taste and an esthetic sense, and an interest in machinery, love of sports and for work. The editors closely follow all new productions of children's plays and include the better ones. A yearly children's program includes some 30 plays, 20–25 special children's films, the *Pioneria* newsreels and animated pictures. Soviet composers and poets and variety artists regularly appear on children's programs. Feature films tell our young spectators about the life and work of heroes of labour and science, about Soviet youth, and adventures of real and fictional heroes. Before showing some films, talks are given by teachers and scientists, or meetings are held with authors, producers and actors of the film.

An important feature of the work of Soviet studios is the exchange of filmed programs. In the larger cities the best stage plays, topical subjects and telecasts are filmed for television studios, which place orders for them. These are sent to all Soviet television centres as well as to other countries. The exchange of television programs between countries contributes to the promotion of relations between their peoples.

V. Sharoyeva

The art of the drama is a problem of communication, not only in time, but about time. At first sight, it seems that this quality belongs to the newer forms of drama: radio, film, and TV. But it is, in fact, of the essence of drama itself, and examples can be found dating back to the earliest history of the art.

Drama, Music, and the Ballet share with Literature the property of moving in time. But in Literature, the creative imagination does not control this movement so fully. The time sense of the private reader, with his power to skip or re-read, is not bound by the creative artist so much as that of the audience of one of the plastic arts.

The dramatist works simultaneously with the Material, the Medium, and the Ground of the drama. The Material of the drama is the world; of reality, or imagination. It may be presented by any means: from writing, or placards, as in film titles, or Elizabethan theater signs; or by direct observation (more or less stylised) as in a silent film sequence, or a passage of mime; or in narration and reflection, as in choruses and soliloquies; or in direct representation by means of actors, or their equivalent (animals, or inanimate objects viewed selectively under creative control); or in any other way that seems effective.

The Medium of the drama is the sum of the qualities of the means of presentation. These qualities may be limitations or advantages, depending upon circumstances and the skill of the dramatist. For example, the quality of the Medium of radio is that the action may be represented only by sounds. This has the limitation of excluding direct visual effects, but the advantage of liberating the audience's visual imagination. In all the arts the Medium is like the sea, which forms the broadest of barriers until the special techniques of navigation have been learned, when it forms the widest of bridges. The dramatic Media include the live stage in all its forms, the radio drama, the film, and live TV drama.

The Ground of the drama is time, upon which the Medium unfolds its Material. Time is the *tabula rasa* on which the dramatist inscribes before our very eyes. Through his Medium, the dramatist arranges his Material in patterns of events in the time sense of the audience. It is the interest of this pattern, as it unfolds, that we call Pace; and the receptiveness to it to which the audience can be stimulated that we call Suspense. The psychological peculiarities of this time sense of the audience should be a constant in the dramatist's calculations. Time that is full of incident seems to pass rapidly, but to be long in retrospect. We are never bored during a crowded exciting day, but in the evening, look back upon the morning, marvelling that it seems so long ago, so much having happened in between. Time, on the other hand, that is empty is slow in passing, but short in retrospect. The prisoner dawdles his slow hours in agonies of boredom; and yet, in retrospect, finds long passages of his life wasted to nothing. The time sense of the audience will respond in the same way to the same sort of stimulation; always remembering that the most important events are those that happen in the heart. Emotional events are the ones that measure time most effectively.

The Material, the Medium, and the Ground are three aspects of the same artistic reality. It is not only improper to separate them; it is impossible. But certain dramatic problems can be clarified by thinking of them as problems of covering the Ground. And these problems again, are but another aspect of the prime artistic problem: that of justly adjudicating the rivals claims of unity and contrast.

In drama, this means arranging the flow of time; in other words developing and maintaining an active sense of pace. Pace should not be confused with speed. There is much more pace in the slow movement of a Mozart than in the most rapid of the studies of Czerny's School of Velocity. Pace is a function of rhythm. In the drama, the rhythm of events on the Ground is determined by the way the Medium orders the events in the Material. Some of these events may be relatively striking: a man and woman fall in love; a child is born; a king is murdered. But even these interesting things can be made boring if there is no interest in the ground that leads up to and includes them. Pace, then, has not been developed. The obvious, consciously effective events may be in good order; the subtle, unconsciously effective events may be chaotic, or almost non-existent.

These unconsciously effective events are far the most numerous in a successful drama. The smallest of them are changes of speech rhythm. In *The Midsummer Night's Dream*, you will find many changes of rhythm, from various kinds of prose, to verse of various structures, some very formal and elaborate. Each of these changes is an event, whether the audience directly perceives it or not. If these events are frequent, the dramatist may have contributed to the effect of contrast; if infrequent, to the effect of unity.

Change of speaker, a second kind of minor event, may reinforce change of rhythm. Stychomathia, the line-for-line exchange of Greek Tragedy, has a pattern of events all of its own. So, for example, does the rapid interchange of the talk about the ghost of Hamlet's father (Act I, Sc. 2). The characteristic pace of the dialogue of Mr Noel Coward, or Mr Ernest Hemingway, is often generated by this device.

In the media of the screen (film and TV), a third kind of minor event, change of shot, can add to the effects of the previous two. The event of the camera's selection, now of the speaker, now of his reacting listener, is an important one.

It is, in fact, a special case of the very important event of change of place; an event which notably stimulates the imagination of the audience. Every change of place is an event, an incident in time, and consequently something added to the pattern on the dramatic Ground. In the media of the screen, change of place very often takes place by change of shot. The juxtaposition and selection of shots is Cutting; and their arrangement is Montage. Most artists in this media would agree with Eisenstein when he says, in *The Film Sense*: 'And now we can say that it is precisely the montage principle, as distinguished from that of representation, which obliges the spectators themselves to create, and the montage principle, by this means, achieves the great power of inner creative excitement in the spectator which distinguishes an emotionally exciting work from one that stops without going further than giving information or recording events.'

He supports this statement about montage in the film with examples from writers such as Pushkin or Milton. Indeed, there are many examples to be found throughout dramatic history. The fluid Elizabethan stage lent itself very much to this kind of event. A good example is *Richard III*,

Act V Sc. 3, when Richard and Richmond are both shown on Bosworth Field, the night before the battle. Both headquarters are shown on the stage at once, and our attention is swayed from one to the other partly by bare alternation, and partly by the movement of the pageant of the ghosts of Richard's murdered victims. The audience is poised between feeling these scenes are rapidly alternating, and that they are simultaneous. The same is true of the fourth act of *Anthony and Cleopatra*, which shows a battle sequence broken into fifteen scenes, one of which (Sc. 11) is only four lines long. In its context, this rapid variation of scene and circumstance gives a very special quality to the pace of the play as it draws towards its denouement. *Woyzeck*, written by Georg Buechner in 1834, takes a slightly different approach. The whole play is divided like this, so that an hour of tragic, violent action is hurried into twenty six short scenes; while Mr. Arthur Miller's *Death of a Salesman* passes at times into an almost continuous flow of change of place, time, mood, or some combination of the three. All these are examples of montage, artistic analogues of screen cutting sequences, and all are powerful ways of generating pace by varying the pattern on the dramatic Ground. Of course, these changes should never be arbitrary; they must mirror fluctuations in the nature of the dramatic Material.

But the dramatist, besides being concerned with the control of time in these indirect but vital ways, is also confronted with time problems in the most direct way. These problems fall into two main groups: first, those having to do with the duration of the action in the Material, and its duration in the Medium, in other words, duration in the world, compared with duration before the audience. Second, those having to do with the manipulation of time to enlarge, complicate and enrich the apparent effect of the Medium.

Duration in the Material and duration in the Medium must necessarily very rarely agree precisely, and usually it is the Material duration which has to be compressed into the Medium duration. The famous debate on Unity of Time was concerned essentially with the degree to which this compression might be theoretically allowed. The orthodox view was stoutly put by Ludovico Castelvetro in his *Opere Varia Critiche* (1570): 'The time of action ought not to exceed the limit of twelve hours. . . . There is no possibility of making the spectators believe that many days and nights have passed, when they themselves obviously know that only a few hours have actually elapsed. They refuse to be deceived.' But they do not refuse to be deceived, in spite of Castelvetro, Cervantes, Sydney, Chapelin, Dryden, Voltaire and many other authorities. On the contrary, while this school is upholding the doctrine of the Unity of Time (in some more or less arbitrary form), another school is denouncing it, by way (among other things) of laying a theoretical foundation for the dramaturgy of Shakespeare. Dr Johnson, having reminded us that if you allow imagination any play whatsoever, you cannot reasonably put arbitrary restrictions on it, goes on to remind us, in sturdy terms, of the basis of theatrical illusion: 'The truth is that the spectators are always in their senses, and know, from the first act to the last, that the stage is only a stage, and that the players are only players. . . . By supposition, as place is introduced, times may be extended; the time required for the fable elapses for the most part between the acts; for, of so much of the action as is represented, the real and poetical duration is the same. . . . Time is, of all modes of existence, most obsequious to the imagination; a lapse of years is as easily conceived as a passage of hours. In contemplation we easily contract the time of real actions, and therefore willingly permit it to be contracted when we only see their imitation.' Again the appeal to the imagination of the audience, for art is always the problem of stimulating and guiding the audience's imagination. The debate on the Unity of Time is now one of the curiosities of the history of the drama, having borrowed from theology, interminability, acrimony, conviction and pointlessness. But though the rule of Unity of Time has been shown by much experience to be senseless when rigidly enforced, and shown by modern authorities (such as H. D. F. Kitto) not to have been the actual practice of those Ancients to whose example the appeal was so often made; nevertheless, the matter is not so cut-and-dried as it might seem. Not only is the question of reconciling duration in the Material and duration in the Medium important, to be ignored only at the dramatist's peril, but also the psychological sense of artistic unity contributed by qualities such as unity of time, is very real, and gives a pungency and point all of its own.

There are a few cases where Material duration and Medium duration correspond exactly. For the most part, these are one-act plays, although Bernard Shaw has tried this solution in *Getting Married*, and in other plays. Even here, many will feel that either there is too much coincidence, or (more important) that the essential movement of emotional events has been speeded up.

Occasionally, the duration of the Material has to be expanded. This rarely happens over the whole work. It is rather over a section of the work. For example, a standard device of the film is intercutting: moving back and forth from one scene to another (as in the fourth act of *Anthony and Cleopatra*). Under suitable circumstances, this may produce the effect that two or more scenes are actually going on simultaneously in different places. If there are two places, the duration of the Material is thus doubled when transformed to the duration of the Medium. Under

71

very special circumstances, the time in the Material may actually come to a complete standstill, while time in the Medium unfolds several events. If, for instance, a man in a TV drama says: 'This woman is a murderer!', we may follow the line of dialogue with a series of close shots of individuals reacting to the idea. If suitably managed, the audience will distinctly feel that these reactions are simultaneous, not consecutive. Time stands still in the Material to allow the Medium to use time to explore the structure of the instantaneous event. Such devices, naturally, produce a singularity in the flow of the pace, and can, therefore, be very useful under skilled control.

Usually, however, the duration of the Material must be compressed, sometimes severely. This may be done smoothly, discontinuously, or irregularly.

A smooth compression of time often takes place within an individual scene. In *Othello*, we find that Act II Sc. 1 contains a storm, a sea-battle, a victory, and the happy landing of the conqueror, all in the space of twenty minutes or so. It is, in fact, usual for the dramatist to heighten and concentrate the Material, and this means compressing its duration, as a rule. While the action is going on, the compression is usually smooth. Any break in the smoothness is a break in the action. Sometimes, however, especially in radio drama it is possible (by means of superimposed narrations) to add sudden leaps to already smoothly compressed scenes.

But discontinuous leaps come, as a rule, between one scene and the next. Sometimes these leaps are very great. Twenty odd years is supposed to pass between the first and second halves of *The Winter's Tale*. Thousands of years are supposed to pass between the various sections of Shaw's *Back to Methuselah*. Audiences are well accustomed to action passing continually but not continuously. In the media of the screen, the presentation is not usually interrupted by an intermission, as in the theater; though it is common to find the scene faded to black, which is the screen equivalent of the radio music cue, or silent break, or the theater's brief curtain, or lowering and raising the lights. In the media of the screen, longer gaps are marked by special devices. These vary from the relative crudity of a clock or calendar, to a montage showing the passage of the seasons, or a recurrent image of some scene charged with emotion and significance.

But the logic of the drama is not the logic of the Schools. Art can always hold in trust, as it were, conflicting ideas and feelings. Most of the masterpieces of art are finely balanced systems of ambivalence. This is particularly true of the drama, with its love of dramatic conflict; and it is even particularly true of dramatic time, so that it may be impossible for cold-blooded analysis to unravel the time scheme of a drama which in performance is eloquent and convincing. Granville Barker's admirable discussion of the double time scheme in *Othello* is perhaps the fullest treatment of a problem of this sort. In short, time in the drama is often used *ad hoc*. This is rationally illogical, but emotionally rigorous. If the dramatist does not find it dramatic to particularise the qualities of the time, then he does not do so. If it is dramatic for some past event to seem very recent; then it is made so to seem. If, a few minutes later, it is dramatic for the same event to seem remote, then that too can be done. If the dramatic reasons were indeed valid, if the Material and the Medium conspired to support the paradox (which may not even be detected, except on close study), then all this will be perfectly acceptable.

There is now the great question of the complication of time; the making of the time of the drama seem richer in texture, and both wider and deeper than it is in reality. It is the quality which a great drama has of seeming to throw out extensions in space and time, so that what is happening has much more general and penetrating meaning than the mere story of a few imagined characters. The way time is complicated is to build into the drama time sequences which lie outside the obvious scope of the Material. As usual, we shall have to divide the indivisible, for the rules of art are rarely either perfectly distinct, or absolutely definite.

The easiest way to expand the material is by means of the Chorus, in the Shakespearean sense, rather than the Greek sense. The Greek chorus is a group of participant spectators. The Chorus in plays such as *Henry V*, tells what we are about to see, or what we must know before the drama can start. This kind of Chorus is much too common in radio, where it is often the lazy man's way out. Notice that it is not the usual time compression involved in fitting the Material to the Medium, because the psychological effect on the audience is quite different. This sort of Chorus, though part of the entertainment, is felt to be outside the drama itself (as in the introduction to *Romeo and Juliet*). Sometimes the Chorus is impersonal, and relatively uncharacterised, as in these examples, or the Chorus at the end of Marlowe's *Dr Faustus*. Sometimes he may be characterised, as when Rumour, Painted Full of Tongues, sets the scene for *Henry IV*, Pt. 2; or ancient Gower sets up *Pericles*. The distinguishing extreme of this means of amplifying the time is that there shall be the promise of action to come, or the rather impersonal tale of action past; but there shall be no action in the present, nor indeed much real sense of action in the past or future. But none the less, this may be a good way of enlarging the time scale with point and brevity.

73

It merges, naturally enough, into the narration of a character, describing in set terms what we have to know, telling what has already happened to himself or to other characters. The curious speeches at the beginning of Chekhov's *Three Sisters* are of this kind. Since the speakers took part in what is described, we have a real sense of action in the past, but, in the extreme, of no action in the present. In any case, the action of the drama is a little enlarged; the straight grain contains an inlay, so to speak. The inlay need not be taken only from the past. It may be from the future; that is to say, a piece of prophecy. There is an example in *Henry VIII*: action in the future, but very little in the present. In Act V Sc. 5, Cranmer begins by prognosticating the entire career of the infant Queen Elizabeth, whom he is holding in his arms, and goes on to praise James I, who could not even be supposed to be a twinkle in his father's eye at the time. In spite of occasional reactions from the other characters, I do not think the audience derives much from this episode in the way of direct action in the scene.

These ways of expanding the time frame merge into the richest and most elaborate situation: where there is not only fresh Material added, but where the new time sequence runs concurrently with the time sequence in the present, so that the Medium is pouring out two streams of time simultaneously. The prophecies of Tiresias in Sophocles' *Oedipus the King* contain (among other fascinating complications of dramatic time) the simultaneous sense of an exciting scene in the present, together with a sense of action to come in the future, to say nothing of a glimpse back into revelations about the past.

Most great playwrights use the interplay of time past and time present as an important device of construction. Ibsen in his maturity, and many others (such as Mr Arthur Miller) use this as their principal device. The Messenger of Greek Tragedy belongs here, as he brings in stunning news, which stimulates his hearers to passionate reaction. Dramas of this sort are elaborately interwoven textures of streams of time; but the important thing is that these different time sequences are not presented alternately but simultaneously. Take, for example, the scene in Ibsen's *Ghosts* when the Rev. Mr Manders, and Mrs Alving discuss the character of the late Captain Alving. Each in turn makes disclosures which are shocking, not only to the other, but to the audience. If a scene like this is wrongly conceived, it will be played as an exchange of reminiscences. What little attention the audience can muster will always be on the speaker, because there is only action in the past. But this is to cripple the dramatic power. There is action in the present as well: before our very eyes. These speeches are not dreamy recollections dredged from the stream of consciousness, but arrows, barbed and poisoned, shot into the other person's heart. As each character speaks, the audience should be attentively watching the other, so that astonishment at the revelations is inextricably bound up with excitement at the reactions they are forcing out.

This technique of simultaneous time is one of the special devices of the drama. Sometimes it may take the form of inset scenes, under circumstances where the main line is sufficiently powerful to keep the main time flow in the audience's attention. For example, in *Hamlet*, there is an inset scene of this kind in the Queen's description of the death of Ophelia (Act IV Sc. 7). In *Henry IV*, Part I; Act I Sc. 3, we find a bitter quarrel between the King and Hotspur, upon which are counter-pointed two inset scenes, both in the form of long speeches by Hotspur. And this counterpoint of time sequences produces something of the effect of musical counterpoint: namely, a sense of total design and order in which the elements partly merge together, and an emotional effect of the whole which is not to be found in the parts taken separately.

Lastly, dramatic irony, in its many aspects, always represents a counterpoint in time. The most useful working definition of dramatic irony is the quality that attaches to a word, a phrase, a speech, an incident, or an episode, by virtue of its context. This definition covers the ordinary use of dramatic irony (where the audience know more than some of the actors); but this implies that the audience is putting the scene into a context which is hidden from the characters. Sometimes this context is entirely within the play, as when we know Hamlet is behind the King as he attempts to pray, and the King does not know it. Sometimes the ironical context is outside the play, and must be supplied from the audience's general background: as in Mr Noel Coward's *Cavalcade*, when the young lovers on the deck of a ship move slowly off arm in arm, to reveal a lifebelt marked, '*Titanic*'.

Eisenstein's remarks about the creative quality of film montage apply here. Dramatic irony stimulates the audience's imagination to creative comparison; and under the right circumstances, the media of the screen can make this stimulation very active. Film montage is continuous, ever-changing dramatic irony, because the value of any shot always partly lies in its relationship to its context, and to that extent is always tinctured with dramatic irony. Dramatic irony is a kind of reverberation in time, so that during the ironic moment many time sequences, both earlier and later are forced simultaneously upon our attention.

Dramatic irony obviously has the same quality; and from one point of view may be thought of as if it were a kind of suburb of the domain of dramatic irony. The simplest metaphor directed to the meanest object suddenly adds to the flow of the play a tiny chip from another world, of another time sequence, in short. The reverberation roused by words like 'Troy' may enrich a scene with dozens of simultaneous associations, or simultaneous time schemes (most of them unconscious). Extended dramatic imagery adds to this invaluable quality the slightly different benefits to be had from the narration of a Chorus. No wonder such images are so effective when they are well used. A good example is in *Hamlet*, Act I Sc. 1, where Horatio compares the present situation in Denmark to the days in Rome before Julius Caesar was assassinated. A very superficial glance shows that these few lines, notoriously powerful in the theater, combine tension in the immediate situation, the association of great and well-known names, much elaborate irony of metaphor, a picturesque counterpoint scene from Antiquity, the idea of apparitions, a conscious foreshadowing of vague disasters to come, and an unconscious, but much more specific foreshadowing of the death of rulers and the fall of great men. All these together form a sort of splendid ornamental knot in the pattern on the dramatic Ground; no wonder the speech strikes so hard and deep.

In recent years, there has been much emphasis (originating with Dr Tyrone Guthrie) on the elements of ritual in the drama. It is undeniable that many plays contain such elements. It is also undeniable that whenever they appear, they necessarily give a quality of dramatic irony, for the essence of a ritual is that we should recognise its familiarity. Perhaps all the characters are aware of the ritual implications. In this case, it is hard to justify the use of the word irony; but certainly as a rule, the characters are carrying out the ritual in a more or less unconscious way. It is the audience that views the whole with heightened awareness, and the sense of endless reduplication of sequences of time.

The art of the drama, then, is, like all the arts, not only a problem of expression, but a problem of communication. But it is a communication not only in time, but about time. This is why the drama is so rich and suggestive, for the details of its technique, as well as its essential function is to stimulate the imagination of the audience, to free them from the necessity of living carelessly as men do, from moment to moment, and to remind them of the beauty and wealth to be found by drawing on experiences in which time is the servant and not the master. This is one of the great factors in the purgation of the emotions that has become such a famous phrase in the theory of tragedy; but the emotions are also purged through comedy, or indeed through any kind of drama. They are made more flexible; the outlook is broadened.

It has been suggested that these qualities of fluid time, of the illusion of simultaneity rather than successiveness, are characteristic of the new mass media: radio, film, TV, and newspapers. The theater should be regarded as one of the mass media, though not a new one. I suggest that these qualities of time are neither new, nor characteristic of the mass media. They are very old (as you will notice from some of the examples), and they are characteristic of the drama. It so happens that all but one of the mass media are in fact dramatic; and the argument from the roving eye that produces the illusion of simultaneity when we scan a newspaper page simply does not apply to the other media. These, in fact, are specially distinguished by their extreme selectiveness. Except on the case of pageants, or pageant-like theatrical productions, the eye (and the attention) is expressly prevented from roving and is carefully directed to the proper place. Radio, film, TV, and the theater are aspects of the drama; and the drama shares with music the quality of arranging time. It is a vital communication whose apparent straightforwardness conceals what is, and always has been, the irresistible fascination of drama: that it is an art form which, for the moment, frees the imagination from the inexorable headlong rush along the one-way street of time.

Lister Sinclair

Though we all know, we often forget, that the existence of America was one of the greatest disappointments in the history of Europe. Plans laid and hardships borne in the hope of reaching Cathay, merely ushered in a period during which we became to America what the Huns had been to us.

C. S. Lewis

Leif Ericson was called 'Leif the Lucky',
not because he discovered a continent four times the size of Europe,
but because he saved some drowning sailors.
Our age has discovered new continents of the mind,
but print's prestige blinds us to them.

We've been darned by giants SOUND asleep
great new media forbidden to realize themselves
while little academic pimps
visit their caprices upon them
and research clowns with buckets of water,
from which they pretend to cast thousands of good-sized fishes,
anathematize us for laughing disrespectfully because,
as with all clowns,
underlying buffoonery is the desire to be taken seriously.

We've been left with corpses and mummies
which twitch and totter with pseudo-life
while pale ignorances,
presiding over tests, instruments, questionnaires,
offer us only wan solemnities.

Dylan Thomas's 'Over Sir John's Hill' merely describes a hawk that kills small birds in the estuary of the river Towy while a heron and a poet watch; something in the descriptive language, rather than any expressed thought or sentiment, makes the scene symbolic and significant. But we have never been certain how much of the significant symbolism was deliberate, how much accidental or a by-product of the poet's seeking lines that sound well. Now the personal history of this poem in forty-seven worksheets, sixty-five written sides, in Harvard Library shows that some phrases were worked and re-worked up to forty-one times; and we are given an opportunity to see exactly what kind of pains Thomas took.

> . . . and again the gulled birds hare
> To the hawk on fire, the halter height, over Towy's fins.

Thomas evidently wants his words to be descriptive and symbolic at the same time. The hawk catches the last rays of the sun and is *on fire*; but the fire is also part of the doomsday-explosion symbolism throughout the poem—by which the hawk becomes a burning gunpowder fuse ready to go off. Thus, the hawk is as much a metaphor for the symbolic fire as the fire is a metaphoric description of the hawk. The poet's effort, represented by the worksheets, is precisely to find the diction that can act this kind of double part, symbolic description and descriptive symbolism.

With *halter height* in the above lines, the symbol-potential perhaps outweighs the descriptive value; a balance is achieved only by combination in the whole phrase *the hawk on fire, the halter height*. This phrase had a particularly long gestation. If my tentative chronology for the worksheets is correct, the hawk of this particular line began as simply *the high hawk*, but then jumped suddenly to a foreshadowing of its final form with *the hempen firing hawk*, both gallows and gunpowder already present. But *hempen firing hawk* did not appear twice; instead we find a more brutal image of slaughter, *the skinning hawk*. Then a new development took place: a single aspect of the hawk, its height, was abstracted and made to stand for the hawk; thus we have *the skinning height* as the place the birds *hare* to. But *skinning* was soon replaced by a reversion to the gallows metaphor, *the hanging height*, and *hanging* in turn intensified to *lynching. The lynching height* appears several times in the drafts (while the poet varies adjacent parts; *e.g., over the river Towy finned* is neatened to *over Towy's fins*) until in one particular three square inches Thomas tries out further alternatives. *Dusky height* is found to have little merit. He picks up the earlier *hempen* and tries *hempen height*, then *hempen caudle height. Caudle* certainly reflects the blithe, *dilly dilly* quality of the small birds' climb to death, the *O.E.D.* giving it as 'a warm drink consisting of thin gruel mixed with wine or ale, sweetened and spiced, given chiefly to sick people, esp. women in childbed'. How true to Thomas's idiom is this passing thought of childbirth linked with death, sweetness with grief. The most interesting thing about the *hempen caudle* metaphor, however, is that it was used by Shakespeare: 'Ye shall haue a hempen Caudle then, and the help of hatchet' (*2 Hen. VI* iv.vii.95). The *O.E.D.* records a second example—from the Marprelate Epistle—of the ironic use of the expression to mean a hanging. What is revealed about the scope of Thomas's reading concerns us here less than the possibility that he discarded *hempen caudle* with all its great pathos primarily because he knew it to be unoriginal. In any case, he reverts to *lynching height* until that stand-by is itself crossed out in favour of *halter height*.

Skinning and *lynching* both implied a vindictiveness that the hawk of the poem does not have. *Hempen* gave an unwanted notion of texture, and failed as a synonym for *noose*—whereas *halter* does not. *Halter* says the same as *hanging*, but more concretely and without syntactical ambiguity. Thomas was looking for the word that would most directly connect us to his gallows symbolism while preserving the amoral, unjudging nature of the death force which the hawk-gallows symbolizes. He eliminated all the words that would make the hawk into anything but an impersonal, universal executioner, essential to mortality and equally to be praised when life is praised.

We realize, too, from following Thomas in his labored movement toward an optimum word-choice, that his words must be rewarding in both sound and meaning. For instance, in the following lines from the poem:

> There
> Where the elegiac fisherbird stabs and paddles
> In the pebbly dab-filled
> Shallow and sedge. . .

we can trust that *sedge* is added to *shallow* for more reason than the good effect of sound, for more reason even than the useful but inconsequential pictorial detail. *Sedge* is marshy grass; but for a second meaning *Funk and Wagnalls* gives: 'A flock of herons or similar birds.' The word is an alternative for *seige*: 'The station of a heron on the watch for prey' (*O.E.D.*). Thomas's heron, then, is not only paddling in the grassy shallows but also in its sedge or seige. The striking subordinate meaning helps the word to deserve its place.

Thomas's intention is evident in the Harvard manuscript: a circled note reads, *Sedge is a lot of herons*; and near it is the phrase *a sedge of heron stilts*, a form the poet did not finally utilize perhaps because, despite its novelty, it is too ready-made. Elsewhere, however, he was having trouble finding a meaningful word to fit a much-favored sound pattern. Throughout the drafts we find the variants: *shallow and shadow, shallow and shade, shallow and stones, shallow and shelves*. His discovery that *sedge* is a word loaded with two suitable meanings, as well as having the desired sound, made *shallow and sedge* the natural end to the search. This phrase, unlike *the hawk on fire, the halter height*, may not add to the serious symbolic theme of the poem; but the very vitality of such description deepens the significance of a song in praise of mortality, which can be said to succeed in so far as the diction vies with life itself in being active and many-sided.

Ralph Maud

The mass media are great manuals of chiropody for feet of clay, anti-bodies for all who are allergic to stardust. During Eisenhower's illness, a communiqué from Denver included the notation that the President had had a good bowel movement. 'I insisted it be put in', Dr. Paul Dudley White, the President's physician, said in *LIFE,* 'because the country will be very pleased. The country is so bowel-minded.'

'For improper thought, a crusher', is *Time's* flippant, insensitive caption beneath the picture of the new Guatemalen chief of police who, under the Ubico dictatorship, 'perfected a head-shrinking steel cap to pry loose secrets and crush improper political thoughts'.

'Blow a little my way, Buddha', says a cigarette ad, and that famous metaphysical smile becomes the smile of the contented smoker.

'And the lambs were there, Ophelia', the lambs being the St. Marys Blanket Company ones, 'there' being the manger in Bethlehem.

NEOTENY AND THE EVOLUTION OF THE HUMAN MIND

A problem perennially puzzling to the student of man has been the manner in which the distinctively human brain and mind have evolved from ape-like counterparts. The mechanism of this evolution has not been understood. Tappen[1] has pointed out that the 'Ancestors of the human group must have made the shift over to symbolic communication in initiate specifically human evolution.' This is reasonably certain. But what is required is some explanation of the mechanism by means of which this shift was achieved. As Tappen adds, 'Once such a shift toward this new adaptive zone was initiated, a high selective advantage for individuals better adapted to learned behaviour and symbolic communication must have ensued.'

Chance and Mead[2] and Etkin[3] have recently proposed some interesting and ingenious theories to explain the shift. The interested reader should consult their papers. In the present paper I shall propose quite another theory.

In a previous contribution[4] I addressed myself to the task of explaining

1 N. C. Tappen, 'A Mechanistic Theory of Human Evolution.' *American Anthropologist,* 55: 605-607.
2 M. R. A. Chance and A. P. Mead, 'Social Behaviour and Primate Evolution.' In *Symposia of Social Experimental Biology,* vii, edited by R. Brown and J. F. Donielli, 395-439.
3 W. Etgin, 'Social Behaviour and the Evolution of Man's Mental Faculties.' *American Naturalist,* 88: 129-142.
4 M. F. Ashley Montagu, 'Time, Morphology, and Neoteny in the Evolution of Man.' *American Anthropologist,* 57: 13-27.

the early appearance of morphologically neanthropic types of men, by an appeal to the process of neoteny. In the present paper I propose to show that the evolution of the human mind probably resulted from the action of the same process.

Neoteny is the process by which the young (fetal and/or juvenile) features of the ancestor are retained in the later postnatal or adult stages of the descendant.

Of all the living creatures man is characterized by the longest learning period. The very duration of this period is of the highest adaptive value, that is *as a learning period*. The prolongation of the learning period in man is clearly a product of evolution, the development of a trait of high selective value. How did this trait come into being?

Let us attempt to return an answer to this question.

The most studied of juvenile apes is the chimpanzee.[1] The evidence of these studies indicates that the active learning period of the juvenile chimpanzee lasts about one year. During this period the juvenile ape develops mentally much more rapidly than the human child of the same chronologic age.

Were the ape infant to maintain its early promise into adolescence it would do very well indeed, but though its early rate of mental development is rapid, that development almost as rapidly comes to a stop. In man mental development is much slower and extended over a much longer period of time. It would seem, then, that in the course of evolution the learning period of the hominids underwent a deceleration in rate and an extension in time, accompanied—evidently—by a corresponding increase in those qualities which make for greater educability.[2]

Is there any demonstrable biological mechanism by means of which such a slowing down of rate of a juvenile trait characteristic of an ancestral form is retained in the descendant? The answer, as I have earlier indicated, is that there is, and that the name which has been given to this mechanism by biologists is *neoteny*. Boas,[3] and in more recent years de Beer[4] have dealt thoroughly with this mechanism as both a developmental and evolutionary process. Pedogenesis, pedomorphosis, and fetalization are terms of practically synonymous meaning. Bolk's[5] theory of

[1] W. N. Kellogg and L. A. Kellogg, *The Ape and the Child;* R. M. Yerkes, *Chimpanzees;* C. Hayes, *The Ape in Our House;* K. J. Hayes and C. Hayes, 'The Cultural Capacity of Chimpanzee.' *Human Biology*, 26: 288-303.
[2] T. Dobzhansky and M. F. Ashley Montagu, 'Natural Selection and the Mental Capacities of Mankind.' *Science*, 105: 587-590.
[3] J. E. V. Boas, 'Ueber Neotenie.' *Festschrift für C. Gegenbaur*, 2:1.
[4] G. R. de Beer, *Embryology and Ancestors.*
[5] L. Bolk, *Das Problem der Menschwerdung;* 'Origin of Racial Characteristics in Man.' *American Journal of Physical Anthropology*, 13: 1-28.

fetalization as applied to the evolution of man is familiar to most anthropologists. Briefly, this is that man has evolved by the preservation of many ancestral fetal characters in the adult. This theory is embraced by the concept of neoteny, which includes the preservation in the adult of juvenile traits.

It is clear that the rate of structural development in man has been appreciably retarded as compared with the rate in apes. It would appear that a similar process was associated with the development of those structural elements which form the physical bases of mind. In other words, as a consequence of neotenous mutations having multiple effects both morphological characters and functional capacities may have been influenced in the hominid-human direction. ('Hominid' refers to the classificatory status of man as a morphological form; 'human' refers to the psychological capacities of such a form). On the other hand the mutations for the strictly morphological changes and those affecting the mental faculties may have occurred quite independently. One thing seems highly probable, namely, that the shift to the human mental status occurred as the result of mutations which caused the retention of the capacity for educability, so characteristic of the juvenile ape, right into the adolescent and/or adult phases of development.

The morphological chasm once separating man from his non-human animal ancestors has been steadily reduced within recent years by the discovery of such extinct forms as the australopithecines of South Africa. Morphologically the australopithecines are not altogether apes (as we have hitherto known them) nor altogether men (as we know them), but something in between—which is exactly what the forms intermediate between apes and the men should be, neither altogether the one (apes) nor quite the other (men), but the advent of the past, so to speak, on its way toward the future. The australopithecines habitually stood and walked erectly as ably or nearly as ably as man. The range of brain volume exceeded that of any known ape group, the largest known ape brain being that of a gorilla with a volume of 685^{cm3},[1] while the australopithecines range in brain volume is 450 to 750^{cm3}.[2] The highest limits of brain volume in the australopithecines fail to fall within the lowest limits of the range of brain volume of modern men of normal intelligence—830^{cm3}.[3]

The brain volume of an australopithecine such as Telanthropus capensis, as estimated by Robinson,[4] namely between 850 and 950^{cm3} is generally

1 A. Hagedoorn, 'Schädelkapazität der Anthropomorphen.' *Anat. Anz.*, 60: 417-427.
2 H. V. Vallois, 'La Capacité Crânienne chez les Primates Supérieurs et le Rubicon Cérébral.' *C. Rend. Séances de l'Acad. des Sciences*, 238: 1349-1351.
3 B. Hechst, 'Uber einen Fall von Mikroencephalie ohne Geistigen Defekt.' *Arch. f. Psychiatrie*, 97: 64076.
4 J. T. Robinson. 'Telanthropus and Its Phylogenetic Significance.' *American Journal of Physical Anthropology*, n.s. 11: 445-501.

agreed to be too high, but 750cm3 is not, and this is within calling distance of the lower limit of the Pithecanthropus-Sinanthropus group with a range of 885 to 1225cm3.[1] Robinson believes that Telanthropus has virtually bridged the gap between ape and man. The gap seems, however, to be larger than Robinson suggests. Most students are of the opinion that the australopithecines do not constitute the group immediately ancestral to man,[2] though most agree that they are closely related to the hominid ancestral group.[3] The cerebral Rubison which Keith placed at a mean of 750cm3 is a good distance from having been crossed by the australopithecines. 'The Rubicon', writes Keith, 'between apehood and manhood, so far as concerns brain volume lies somewhere between 700 c.c. and 800 c.c.; to be more precise, I would say that any group of the great Primates which has attained *a mean brain volume* of 750 c.c. and over should no longer be regarded as anthropoid, but as human.' The emphasis here is upon *a mean brain volume*, and the mean brain volume of the australopithecines is 576cm3.[4] This is quite a long way from the mean brain volume of the pithecanthropoids of 881cm3. On the basis of brain volume the australopithecines have not crossed the Rubicon to achieve the status of man.

A point of great significance is that the human brain begins its real growth and development at birth, and continues to grow and develop in the functions of a human being, throughout the first two decades of life. The brain of a 3 year old child is almost of the size and weight of that of an adult. By the age of 6 years the brain has generally almost achieved full adult size. In man the active growth of the brain far exceeds that of any other primate. At birth the mean weight of the brain in caucasoids is approximately 350 gm or approximately 3.9 times less than its adult weight. The growth of the brain is very different from that of the rest of the body, being quite explosive during the first year when it more than doubles to a weight of 750 gm—a gain of 400gm. In the second year the gain is almost 200gm, in the third year about 100gm, and at the latter rate up to the end of the fifth year when the brain weight reaches 1230gm. From the sixth to the tenth year the increment varies as follows: 19gm between 5 and 6 years, 8gm between 6 and 7 years, 46gm between 7 and 8 years, and 10gm between 9 and 10 years. After the first decade and to the end of the second decade the increment is less than 3gm a year—to a total of 1373gm.[5]

At birth the human brain is only 23 per cent of its adult size, and by the end of the first year the human infant has achieved 55 per cent of its

1 Vallois, *op. cit.*
2 K. P. Oakley, 'Dating the Australopithecinae of South Africa.' *American Journal of Physical Anthropology*, n.s. 12: 9-23.
3 W. E. Le Gros Clark, 'Reason and Fallacy in the Study of Fossil Man.' *Discovery*, 16: 6-15.
4 E. H. Ashton, 'The Endocranial Capacities of the Australopithicinae.' *Proceedings of the Zoological Society of London*, 120: 715-721; Vallois, *op. cit.*
5 K. D. Blackfan, ed., *Growth and Development of the Child*, pt. 2, Anatomy and Physiology.

total brain growth; by the end of the third year some 83 per cent. In the great apes the major part of the growth is achieved within the first year. In the rhesus monkey and in the gibbon 70 per cent of the brain growth has been achieved by birth, and the remainder is completed within the first six months. In the great apes the active period of brain growth occurs during the first eleven months, and in man during the first thirty-six months. Complete growth of the brain in man is not achieved until the end of the second decade of life. As Keith has pointed out, in this prolongation of cerebral growth and development we see an important, 'if not the most important, feature of human evolution— namely, the time taken to assemble and to organize the myriads of nerve cells and of nerve tracts which enter into the structure of man's brain.' This process, as Keith adds, exemplifies the 'law' of fetalization or neoteny, and it is this process which is capable of explaining the evolution of that most unique of all traits, the human mind.

It seems reasonably clear that the growth (increase in size) and development (increase in complexity) of the human brain is a neotenous phenomenon. In other words, man preserves something akin to the rate of growth and development characteristic of the fetal brain or preserves and improves upon the rate of growth and development of the infant ape-brain long after the latter has ceased to grow.

It can be taken as fairly well established that the evolution of the brain in man is associated with his remarkable mental faculties.[1] It would seem highly probable that the great adaptive value of a brain endowed with such potentialities was responsible for the natural selection and preservation of those individuals in whom such neotenous mutations had occurred or had been transmitted.

It does not seem that many great structural changes would be necessary to produce those qualitative changes that would serve to distinguish the human from the ape mind. It would seem, on the other hand, that the principal, if not the only changes necessary would be those facilitating the ease of symbol usage. What the nature of those changes may be is at present conjectural. Increase in the number of fine connections between cerebral neurons with increased capacity for growth at axon terminals, resulting in improvement in the association, scanning, and feedback capacities of the brain, is one possibility. Thorndike[2] has suggested that 'in their deeper nature the higher forms of intellectual operation are identical with mere association or connection forming, depending upon the same sort of physiological connections but requiring many more of them.' This is possibly an oversimplification. However we may describe

---

[1] H. J. Jerison, 'Brain to Body Ratios and the Evolution of Intelligence.' *Science*, 121: 447-449.
[2] E. L. Thorndike, M. C. Bregman, and E. Woodyard, *The Measurement of Intelligence.*

the structural changes which have undoubtedly taken place in the human brain, they will amount to but the other aspect of what we have already stated, namely, that the difference between the human and ape brain is that the human is more educable. Indeed, educability is the species characteristic of *Homo sapiens*. The juvenile ape is more educable than the adult ape, and the suggestion here is that the preservation of the educability of the juvenile ape into the adult stage in man, by neoteny, serves to explain the evolution of a brain capable of a human mind.

The theory proposed in the present paper suggests that the shift from the status of ape to the status of human being was the result of neotenous mutations which produced a retention of the growth trends of the juvenile brain and its potentialities for learning into the adolescent and adult phases of development. It is clear that the nature of these potentialities for learning must also have undergone intrinsic change, for no amount of extension of the chimpanzee's capacity for learning would yield a human mind.

It is further suggested that evolution by neoteny of the mental faculties has been a gradual process from the commencement of man's origin from the apes. It is questionable whehter the shift from the ape to the hominid status was saltatory either for morphological or for mental traits. It may be doubted, for example, that Pithecanthropus robustus was as bright as Solo man, though it is highly probable that he was brighter than any of the australopithecines. The progressive increase in the volume of the brain in the fossil Hominidae seems to have been paralleled by a progressive increase in mental capacities. Size of brain seems to have stabilized itself in man,[1] in fact there seems to have been a decline in gross size of the human brain since the days of Neanderthal man. This does not, however, mean that the increase in brain volume has come to an end. As is well known, increase in volume may be achieved by deepening and multiplication of the number of cerebral convolutions, that is, by increasing the surface area of the brain without increasing its size. There is no reason to suppose that either the quality or duration of man's capacity for learning will not be subject to further evolution.

M. F. Ashley Montagu

---

[1] G. von Bonin 'On the Size of Man's Brain as Indicated by Skull Capacity.' *J. Comp. Neurol.*, 59: 1-29; W. E. Le Gros Clark, 'Observations on Certain Rates of Somatic Evolution in the Primates.' In *Robert Broom Commemorative Volume.* Special Publication of the Royal Society of South Africa.